THE ALTARPIECE

All the scenes on the altarpiece except two – the Assumption and th
Eugenius – depict episodes from the life, passion and glory of Christ.
focuses on the importance of the Virgin Mary, Mother of God, the two crucial moments in the life of Christ – His Nativity and Death – and the Blessed Sacrament of the Eucharist. The chronological order of the scenes is as follows:

Childhood of Christ: 7, 3, 15, 16, 8

Passion of Christ: 14, 6, 18, 11, 12, 13, 5, 9

Glorious Life of Christ: 17, 21, 20, 19

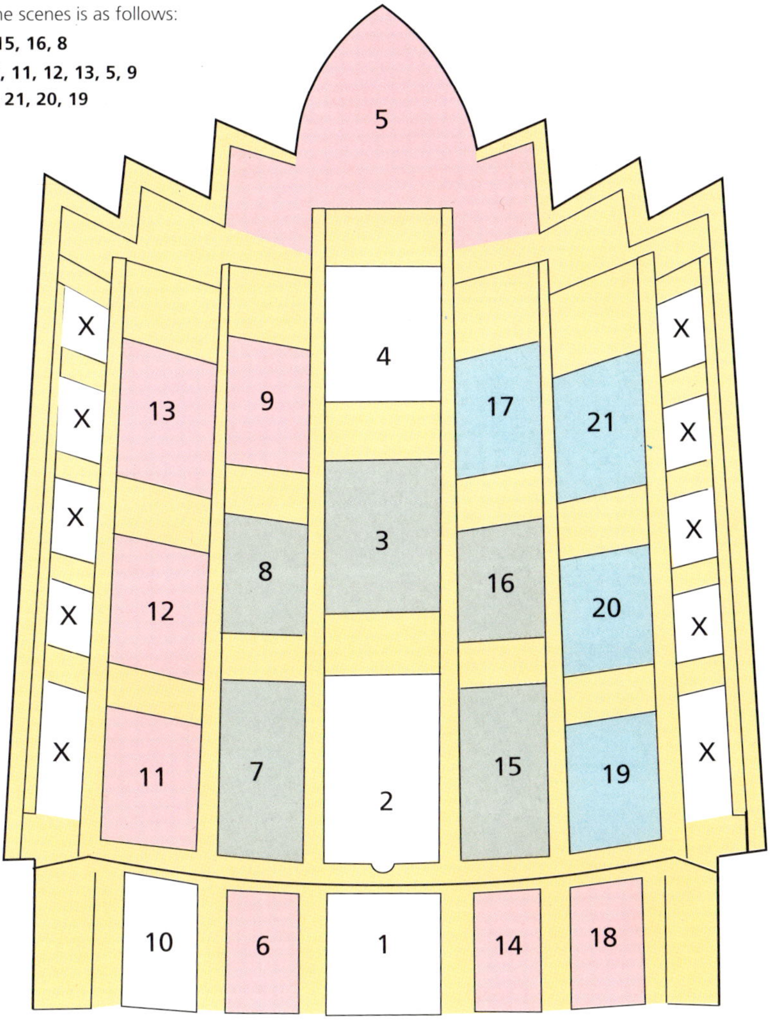

1 The Virgin and Child
2 The Sacrarium of the Blessed Sacrament
3 The Nativity of Jesus
4 The Assumption of the Virgin, which occupies a privileged position as the Cathedral is dedicated to this mystery in the life of the Mother of God
5 The Crucifixion
6 The Last Supper
7 The Annunciation
8 The Circumcision of Christ
9 The Descent from the Cross
10 The Beheading of St Eugenius, first archbishop of Toledo. Its inclusion on the altarpiece is an allusion to the apostolic continuity between Christ and the hierarchy, represented here by a martyr who suffered in the example of the Passion of the Saviour.
11 The Flagellation of Christ
12 Ecce Homo (Christ Presented to the People)
13 Christ on the Way to Calvary
14 The Washing of Feet
15 Epiphany, or Adoration of Christ by the Magi
16 The Slaughter of the Innocents
17 The Resurrection of Christ
18 Prayer in the Garden
19 The Last Judgement
20 Pentecost, or the Coming of the Holy Spirit
21 The Ascension of Christ
X Prophets and patriarchs

Legal Deposit: M-43840-1997
I.S.B.N. 84-8003-084-4
Design and Layout: Juan Manuel Domínguez and Rose Mayer
Coordination: © ALDEASA ®
Photographs: Juan Manuel Domínguez, Oronoz*
Photomechanical production: Lucam
Translation: Nigel Williams

Printed in Spain by Estudios Gráficos Europeos

(Printed in Spain)

GUIDE TO

TOLEDO CATHEDRAL

José Luis Sancho

CONTENTS

HOTEL

TOLEDO CATHEDRAL, PRIMATE SEE OF SPAIN

The Cathedral in Toledo's history

The importance of Toledo in the history of Spain and the influence of religion on Spanish art and culture are symbolized in Toledo Cathedral, See of the Archbishop Cardinal Primate of Spain. Upon its site a Visigothic basilica once witnessed some of the famous Councils of Toledo. Its first bishop, at the end of the 1st century, was St Eugenius, but the most famous of all was St Ildefons, defender of the virginity of Mary. According to tradition, on 18th December 666 (possibly one year before or after), the Virgin came down to the high altar and invested her devotee with a chasuble. This scene — *La Descensión* ("The Descent") — which is the Cathedral's emblem dedicated to the Virgin Mary, is to be found everywhere in the building. Although this miracle is believed to have taken place on 18th December, it is celebrated on 24th January, the day after the saint's feast.

Recent excavations beneath the first three sections led to the discovery of the Visigothic foundations on a Greek cross ground plan with a presbytery next to the altar of La Descensión (built to mark the place where the miracle occurred). It was only after the 8th century and more particularly after the 13th, that the miracle was more widely referred to in church literature.

For 370 years (714-1085) Toledo was an Islamic city: the main mosque was originally situated next to what is now the east side of the Cathedral but later incorporated the Visigothic building. Successive alterations and extensions in the 10th and 11th centuries produced a prayer hall 60 metres by 40 covering almost all the sections of the Cathedral as it stands today, from the west end to the crossing (eleven sections). The mihrab was more or less where the Puerta Llana doorway now stands, and the courtyard covered part of the present-day cloisters. Of this building an engaged capital remains (in the Chapel of Santa Lucía), as do various 10th-century columns which were reused in the construction of the retrochoir (see p. 28).

When Alfonso VI conquered Toledo in 1085, the capitulation guaranteed that the mosque would continue to be a place of Muslim worship. However, while the king was absent in October 1087, Queen Constance and Archbishop Bernard, a Cluny monk, had the building reconsecrated as a Christian church. In spite of this action, the Alfaqui or Ulema, Abu-Walid, dissuaded the Muslims from confronting the queen, and instead placated the king, despite the broken promise.

Little more than a century later the old mosque had become too old and unsuitable for use as a place of worship by an opulent religion so different from that of Islam. Toledo had by then the richest see in

TOUR OF THE NAVE, SIDE AISLES AND CHAPELS

This tour of the Cathedral concentrates on the chapels and inner faces of the doorways as indicated by the numbers on the plan. Also described here, although not indicated on the plan, are the small altarpieces on the pillars in the nave and side aisles. Each pillar was associated with a specific altarpiece until 1500, when Cisneros had the altar tables removed as they were considered a hindrance; from then on and until the 19th century, portable altars were set up for mass in front of saints' altars or "stations" on their feast days. These small altarpieces were much larger in number before general alterations were made between 1789 and 1791, when some were removed or replaced by statues set into the walls of the choir and in the Chapel of Santiago or by paintings with rich marble frames also set into the walls.

As the Cathedral's very rich stained-glass windows are worthy of a guide of their own, here we shall discuss only their iconographic and artistic importance. The rose window in the north façade dates from the 14th century. The windows of the Main Chapel and the east area of the crossing date from the middle of the 15th century and were made by Masters Delfín and

The Descent, a copy of Saraceni's work by Aguirre, in the antechapel to the Sacrarium.

A detail from the stained-glass windows above the Puerta del Perdón.

Luis, while those in the west wall of the crossing above the nave date from the second half of the 15th century and are by Pedro Bonifacio. The south rose window and many others (plus repairs) were made in the 16th century by Juan de la Cuesta, Vasco de Troya, Alejo Jiménez, Juan de Campos, Alberto de Holanda, Juan Ortega and the Vergaras, to name only a few of the oldest masters of a craft which continued to exist until the 18th century.

1. The Altar de la Descensión abutting the second pillar between the two side aisles is, despite its rather eccentric position, the Cathedral's true gem as this was the original site of the high altar in the Visigothic basilica, and also where, according to local tradition, the miracle of the "descent of the Queen of Heaven" to bestow the chasuble upon the Bishop, St Ildefons, took place. Because of this Henry II decided to create the burial Chapel of Reyes Nuevos in this corner of the Cathedral "before the pillar where trod the Virgin"; the chapel was transferred (see p. 40) and consequently around 1540 the altar as it is today was made. It had a marble baldachin

the Peninsula and was the seat of the Archbishop Primate of a safe, expanding kingdom. Furthermore, by the time Ferdinand III — who conquered Seville in 1226 and succeeded in uniting the crowns of Castile and León in 1230 — decided to erect a new cathedral in Toledo, Almoravid raids and Almohad power had become things of the past.

The cathedral's architecture and the story of its construction

Consequently, the king ordered the construction of a great Gothic cathedral similar to those in France but in accordance with Hispanic tastes. The result of such a synthesis and of the process of construction, which lasted until the end of the 15th century (the last vaults being completed in 1493), was a fascinating building of granite and white Olías stone.

In 1224 the preparation of the plot (purchased especially) was begun and the foundation stone was laid on 14th August 1226. Work continued for 265 years.

The initiative came from Jiménez de Rada, Archbishop Primate (1209-1247) and a man of international repute who had studied at the nascent University of Paris, journeyed to Rome and had dealings with four popes. A defender of the rights of the Christian church, he was a counsellor to Alfonso VIII, Doña Berenguela and Ferdinand III, during whose reigns he played a crucial role. Fully aware that architecture is one expression of

(Left) the Chapel of La Descensión with its altarpiece by Felipe Bigarny.

Stained-glass windows in the nave; detail, the complete window.

View of the nave from the Puerta del Perdón.

surmounted by pinnacles, buttresses and Flamboyant Gothic crenellation that almost certainly date from the late-15th century and presumably came from another part of the Cathedral. In 1610 J. B. Monegro widened the steps and to close the pointed openings made new grilles with the remains of Plateresque grating, in all likelihood made by Domingo de Céspedes in 1525. The magnificent alabaster altarpiece within was made (and signed) by Felipe Bigarny but as he died before it was completed, the work was finished by his son Gregorio Pardo. It consists of: the *Descent* in the centre; the *Four Fathers of the Christian Church* at the sides; and, in the attic, the *Assumption*. The predella around the sacrarium contains beautiful reliefs of the *Annunciation*, the *Visitation*, the *Nativity*, the *Appearance of St Leocadia* and the *Sermon of St Ildefons*. Here also is the gravestone of Cardinal Moscoso (d. 1655), who financed the frontal, made by Fanelli and Salinas (c. 1668), which bears his portrait and coats of arms (in bronze).

The interior face at the west end of the Cathedral and the doors known as the Puerta del Perdón, Puerta del Juicio and Puerta de los Escribanos (see p. 54) stand five steps higher than the floor inside and two below the porch. In addition to the large rose window with the Tavera coat of arms in the centre, it displays two small altarpieces, one being that of St Joseph, by Alonso del Arco, and the other of an anonymous, 17th-century Immaculate Conception. Over the Puerta de los Escribanos an inscription commemorates the conquest of Granada and the expulsion of the Jews in 1492, and the completion of work on the Cathedral in 1493, when Mendoza was Cardinal. The stained-glass window above displays the coat of arms of Fonseca. Above the pillar opposite the Puerta de los Escribanos and to the left is a sculpture of *Christ at the Column* by Olarte (1523) on a small alabaster altarpiece dating from the time of Fonseca and therefore somewhat later than it. On the pillars of the nave are four more small altarpieces.

2. The Capilla Mozárabe. During the Muslim domination of Toledo Christian worship continued to be led in six parish churches and a number of hermitages according to the old Visigothic rite. After Alfonso VI conquered Toledo, the descendants of the Mozarabs

power, Rada determined to raise a French Gothic church worthy of the aspirations of a metropolitan see located within a Mudéjar Castile tinged with Muslim influences. Furthermore, he succeeded in making his main chapel a burial place of kings.

The Cathedral's first architect and also its designer was Master Martín, from his name and work apparently a Frenchman. The large ground plan of five sections (120 meters long by 60 wide) whose double ambulatory was ingeniously built with alternating rectangular

and triangular spans, is similar to those of the cathedrals of Paris, Bourges and Le Mans.

However, it is the spirit of Toledo that pervades the cathedral. Although a perfect Gothic work, the ambulatory reflects the influence of the Almohad architecture of Seville. The proportions of the ground plan are very different from those of the French cathedrals, for it is comprised of two circles, one formed by the ambulatory, the other by the rest of the area, the length of the two being twice the breadth. Furthermore, the crossing is not situated at the centre, as in the case of Paris or Burgos, but much closer to the east end. More strikingly different from the French style are the elevations, which are much less slender. Moreover, the outermost side aisles are broader than those closest to the middle, which heightens the sense of serenity in the interior. Indeed it could be said that the site of the mosque passed on part of its horizontal spaciousness to the Christian building.

Mudéjar influence is evident in certain details of the ambulatory and the Main Chapel — the first part to be built and the area in which the greatest peculiarities in the elevations appear (such as the triforia

The ambulatory with the Transparente and the Chapels of Santiago and San Ildefonso.

(Christian subjects of Islam) resisted the introduction of the Roman or Gregorian rite which Archbishop Bernardo and Queen Constanza wished to impose. The king was therefore forced to permit the Gothic rite in these parishes, although he did all in his power to encourage the Roman rite. Thus there emerged the mixed *Toledo rite* used during worship in the Cathedral until 1574, when the Council of Trent imposed the Roman rite. By the beginning of the 16th century it seemed that the *Mozarabic rite* would be lost as the congregations at the six churches were dwindling. In order to preserve it Cardinal Cisneros created this chapel and the rite has continued to be used here until the present day, with the Mozarabic mass being said on Saturday mornings at 9.30 a.m. On this site stood the old Chapter House and a chapel devoted to the

Corpus Christi. For the construction of the new chapel Cisneros was obliged to purchase the premises from the Chapter and finance a new Chapter House (see p. 35).

Directed by Enrique Egas, the work was under way by 1502 and had virtually reached completion by 1510, although as early as 1504 it was being used for worship. Juan de Arteaga and Francisco de Vargas built a lantern (designed by Egas) between 1511 and 1519 to replace the provisional roof covering. However, it was destroyed by fire in 1622 and rebuilt by Theotocopoulus, who completed it in 1631 (see p.p. 55, 57).

The Gothic doorway displays tracery painted by Juan de Borgoña, a *Pietà* ascribed to Enrique Egas, and a screen by Juan Francés (1524). On either side of the entrance are small altarpieces of gilded wood dating from the beginning of the 17th century and depicting *St Nicholas of Tolentino* and *The Stigmata of St Francis*. The latter was financed by Francisco de Pisa, the Mozarabic chaplain and Toledo historian (who died in 1616 and is buried at its side).

On the right is the altar. The original altarpiece was designed by Francisco de Amberes

View of the inner face of the Puerta del Perdón, at the west end of the Cathedral.

with their Hispano-Arabic trefoil arches). This blend heightens the fascination of the apse, planned in accordance with the mystic symbology of Gothic architecture: the fifteen chapels of the ambulatory consecrated in 1238 and surrounding the Main Chapel (a replica of the Holy Sepulchre, see p. 30), were dedicated to each of the articles of the Creed as related to the apostles; the Cathedral, the mystical image of the Celestial City, was further enriched by references to the Holy City and the Temple of Solomon.

After Master Martín we know that Petrus Petri (or Pedro Pérez, d. 1285) led the work on the Cathedral ; however we do not knowthe names of those who succeeded him in the late-13th and early-14th centuries. In the mid-1300s Cardinal Gil de Albronoz introduced Italian influence which intensified in the last thirty years or so of the century during the productive pontificate of his admirer, Archbishop Pedro Tenorio. The Archbishop's architect, Rodrigo Alfonso, built (among many other things) the cloisters, beginning them in 1389. In the 15th century Master Alvar Gómez, or González, who erected most of the main façade and the towers, was succeeded as chief architect or master builder by various Flemish and French builders who brought Northern European influence to Toledo. It seems that a certain Hanequín Egas (or Hanequin of Brussels) had settled in Seville, where Juan de Cerezuela was archbishop; when Cerezuela was transferred to Toledo, Egas accompanied him and worked on the Cathedral during the middle third of the 15th century.

Martín Sánchez Bonifacio, also from Seville, worked on the Cathedral from 1448; he was promoted to master builder in 1470 and held this post until 1490. Sánchez was succeeded by Juan Guas from Brittany, a qualified stone-mason who had begun working in Toledo on the Puerta de los Leones. As master mason from 1458 he carried out a vast amount of highly personal work, especially between 1470 and the end of the century. On his death the Egas family became prominent in the construction of the Cathedral: Egas Cueman, a younger brother of Hanequín's, was first chief sculptor, later one of the Cathedral's quantity surveyors, and finally, on the death of Guas, became master builder His two sons, Antón and Enrique Egas, became distinguished architects who also worked on the Cathedral.

Construction ended in the time of Cardinal Mendoza, but his successors, the extraordinary 16th-century Archbishops Cisneros, Tavera, Silíceo... enriched the Cathedral with further admirable works. The 17th century saw the creation of the Sagrario and Ochavo chapels, the Sacristy and its adjacent buildings, and the 18th the Baroque ostentatiousness of the *Transparente*, a large-scale general renovation of the Cathedral, and the addition of numerous Neo-Classical works.

The complexity of the inner spaces and the colour and richness of the decoration are what differentiate the strong character of Spanish

cathedrals from the greater sobriety of their counterparts in other European countries. In Toledo Cathedral the effect of its accumulated treasures is much more striking than in any other building of this kind, for the innumerable altars (at which more than *thirty-six thousand masses* were celebrated each year), the chapels founded by prominent persons, the altarpieces, the tombs, the adjacent buildings necessary for keeping the vestments in, and the attendance of the countless higher and lower members of the clergy prove how appropriate was the name "The Rich" by which the Cathedral was known in the Middle Ages: *Dives Toletana*. In 1086, Alfonso VI granted the chapter and the archbishop a very generous endowment; the diocese was the largest in Spain, and divine worship took place there with a degree of ostentatiousness and magnificence that is hard to imagine today.

The Battle of Oran, by Juan de Borgoña, a fresco in the Capilla Mozárabe.

Disembarkation of Cisneros in Oran, by Juan de Borgoña, a fresco in the Capilla Mozárabe.

THE AREAS OF WORSHIP WITHIN THE CATHEDRAL

The principal places for worship — the Main Chapel and the choir — stand in the centre of the building. They face each other across the transept, so that the area is divided up in the manner commonly found in Spanish cathedrals.

and painted by Borgoña and Villoldo, but Cardinal Lorenzana commissioned another Neo-Classical one of various types of marble (1791). What remains of this is the *Virgin with the Child Triumphant*, a magnificent 18th-century Roman mosaic copied from a painting by Carlo Maratta. The present altarpiece dates from 1924, although it contains Gothic panels of the *Last Supper* and various Saints dating from the 15th century and originally from the old Synagogue of El Tránsito. Above this is a crucifix of fennel wood from the Americas (1590). The small side altarpieces are Gothic.

On the left and opposite the altar is the chaplains' choir with Medardo Arnot's Neo-Classical stalls of rare woods. The grille by Eulogio Dueñas is modern, although the base of the eagle lectern dates from the 15th century. The stained-glass windows were made by Juan de la Cuesta in 1513.

On the wall opposite the entrance are three fresco Scenes from the *Conquest of Oran* by

The tombs of Alfonso VII "The Emperor" and Doña Berenguela, in the Main Chapel (Right).

View of the dome in the Capilla Mozárabe, by Egas and Jorge Manuel Theotocopoulus.

THE MAIN CHAPEL

This area owes its present appearance (1498-1504) to Cardinal Cisneros, but parts of it date from previous periods. Until the end of the 15th century it was limited to the rectangular section between the screen and the steps leading up to the presbytery, for the area corresponding to the polygonal vault at the sanctuary was the site of the old Chapel of La Santa Cruz, a royal pantheon founded by Sancho the Brave (p. 30). In 1498 Cisneros persuaded the Catholic Kings to transfer the area dedicated to prayer for the souls of these "Old Kings" to a new chapel at the side (see p. 30), so as to enlarge the Main Chapel, which had become too small for all the members of the clergy who assembled there on solemn feast days.

But the *Royal Tombs* remained on both sides of the new altarpiece: here lie Alfonso VII the Emperor (left), his sons Sancho the Desired and Sancho the Brave (right), all with long robes and swords. However, the statue of prince Pedro de Aguilar — son of Alfonso XI and Leonor de Guzmán — (left) does not carry weapons as he died at eight years of age. Two other princes named Sancho — both Archbishops of Toledo — also lie here; as does Sancho the Cowled, fourth king of Portugal, who died in Toledo in 1248.

The statues are the original ones, as, possibly, are their positions, raised above an opening with a grille decorated in Mendoza's time on the ambulatory side (see p. 30) under a low arch with the royal coats of

The Main Chapel from the south transept with Villalpando's screen and the Santa Lucía wall.

Details from the High Altarpiece. On the left, the Martyrdom of St Eugenius. On the right, The Last Supper by Felipe de Borgoña (1498-1504).

Juan de Borgoña, painted almost contemporarily (1514) to the event, while Cisneros was still alive; a refuge for pirates in North Africa, Oran was taken in 1509 by the Cardinal and governor himself, just as the scene of the *Disembarkation* depicts on one of the sides; on the other side is the *Embarkation of the Expedition in Cartagena,* and, in the centre, the *Conquest of Oran*.

In the first section of the side aisle, in semicircular niches next to the Capilla Mozárabe, are two tombs of Archdeacons. They were carved by Alonso de Covarrubias in 1514.

From this point on all the chapels on this side were endowed and decorated in the early years of the 16th century by rich members of the Chapter who wished to follow Cisneros's example when he founded the Capilla Mozárabe.

3. The Chapel of La Epifanía is a beautiful Gothic composition dating from the late-15th and early-16th centuries. Behind the screen, by Juan Francés, and under a groined vault with pendants displaying thistles is the magnificent altarpiece, ascribed to Juan de Borgoña. In the lower section is the *Entombment*; in the centre, *St John the Baptist*, the *Adoration of the Magi*

arms beneath it. The Flamboyant Gothic baldachins, designed and worked by Copín (1507) and painted and gilded by Juan de Arévalo, however, date from the time of Cisneros; the angels in flight bear the coats of arms of the Catholic Kings.

Work on the grandiose larch-wood *altarpiece* designed by Petit Jean was directed (1498-1504) by Enrique Egas and Pedro Gumiel. Petit Jean also carved the ornamentation in the sanctuary, the pillars and the canopies. His large team included Francisco de Aranda, Diego de Llanos, Diego de Guadalupe, Lucas Salas and Antonio Frías. The scenes of the *Life and Passion of Christ* were carved by Felipe de Borgoña (the four in the lower section), Diego Copín and Sebastián de Almonacid, all of whom also worked on the *Calvary* above; the latter is huge, for the higher the figures the larger their proportions.

Gilded and painted by Francisco de Amberes and Juan de Borgoña, it was completed in 1504, the same year as the death of Isabella the Catholic. Of the large altarpieces common in late 15th-century Spain, this one, together with those in Seville, Oviedo and Orense, is among the most important.

The presbytery, which contains the altarpiece and the royal tombs, stands nine steps above the rest of the Main Chapel. The steps are flanked by the *pillars of the Shepherd and the Alfaqui* (Ulema).

The Pillar of the Shepherd, to the left of the High Altarpiece, depicts the person who led Alfonso VIII's army via a short-cut to Navas de Tolosa, thus ensuring a victory crucial for the continuation of Christian domination in Castile. Because of this the shepherd was later identified

(Above) Prayer in the Garden, by Felipe de Borgoña, on the High Altarpiece (1498-1504).

(Left) The High Altarpiece (1498-1504) with sculptures by Felipe de Borgoña, Diego Copín and Sebastián de Almonacid.

as an angel, or as St Isidore Labrador ("the Farmer"). The image was placed here in gratitude, with the robe down to the feet, the hood over the head and crook in hand, just as the king (whose effigy is directly above), remembered the shepherd.

The Ulema on the pillar on the right was also placed here in gratitude, in this case to the dignitary of the Muslim community of Toledo who dissuaded his people from demanding that Alfonso VI allow

and *St James;* and in the upper section, *Calvary, St Peter* and *St Paul*. Above these are painted marble statues of the *Virgin and St John the Evangelist*. The frontal is of slate. To the left a tomb dating from the transitional period from Gothic to Renaissance is the resting place of Canon Luis Daza (1504), who endowed and adorned this chapel exactly as it is today — as is indicated in a framed inscription within an ogee arch.

4. The Chapel of La Purísima Conception is also very consistent and again dates from the time of the transition from Gothic to Renaissance. The screen is ascribed to Francés; the groined vault has gilded pendants. The altarpiece, with Flamboyant Gothic decoration between the panels and attic by now displaying motifs of Renaissance candleholders, is ascribed to Francisco de Amberes. In the first section are *SS. Peter and Paul, a Pietà with St John and Mary Magdalene* and *St John the Baptist with St*

(Left) The Washing of Feet by Felipe de Borgoña, on the High Altarpiece (1498-1504).

(Right) The tomb of Cardinal Mendoza in the Main Chapel (c. 1495-1500).

Antony; in the second section, the *Birth of the Virgin*, the *Conception (The Embrace Before the Golden Gate)*, and the *Adoration of the Magi;* the third section contains the *Annunciation*, the *Visitation* and the *Nativity*. Above this is a carved crucifix, with the coat of arms of the chapel's founder. In the left wall is a tomb with a recumbent effigy (by Vasco de la Zarza's circle), marking the resting place of Canon Juan de Salcedo, who endowed and adorned this chapel in 1502. In the arcosolium there is a coloured alabaster *St John the Evangelist* dating from the 16th century.

5. The Puerta Llana takes its name ("Flat Door") from the fact that it is the only entrance at street level. It was also known as: Puerta de los Carretones ("Door of the Carts"), as building materials were brought through it during work on the Cathedral; and Puerta del Deán, because the Dean's house was opposite it. The beautiful

Toledo's Main Mosque to be rededicated as a Muslim place of worship after its violent consecration as a cathedral by Bishop Bernard and Queen Constance.

The sculptures on each of the pillars they are named after were the closest ones to the wall in the old Main Chapel until 1498, but when the wall was demolished four statues of kings (taken from the left-hand side of the chapel's rectangular section) were added to each one.

The original screen on the left-hand side was identical to that on the right. The latter, known as the *Screen of St Lucy,* is a beautiful work dating from the late-14th century. Consisting of eight arches on slender marble columns, it allowed the congregation to follow the services from the first sections of the ambulatory. On the second level there are eight almost life-size archbishops, and above these two rows of smaller-sized saints in quatrefoil recesses; all is surmounted with cresting containing angels. On the outside are apostles instead of prelates.

It seems that the sculptures in the second section of each screen and those on the pillars running towards the crossing originally formed the series of archbishops and Castilian monarchs who governed during the time of the Cathedral's construction; as there was not enough room for them inside the Main Chapel, they were placed along the outer pillars of the transept. Their ornamentation dates from the time of Alonso Carrillo (c. 1460), the last of the archbishops depicted (where for the sake of symmetry archbishops alternate with saints).

Identical to the one on the right (that of St Lucy), the left-hand

The transept from the Puerta del Reloj with the Puerta de los Leones in the background.

screen in the Main Chapel was demolished (according to local tradition in the course of a single night) against the Chapter's will but on the insistence of Isabella I, who as Archbishop Mendoza's (d. 1495) executrix carried out this *Cardinal of Spain's* last wish. This important prelate of the Spanish Renaissance had made generous donations to the Cathedral and in exchange wished to be buried in its place of honour, to the right of the high altar. Thus, in the place of the Gothic screen a grandiose *tomb* was built (c. 1495-1500). Inspired by the works of Sansovino and ascribed to Domenico Fancelli and his team of Genoese marble-workers, it was of prime importance in the spread of Italian Renaissance taste in Spain. It is set out in the manner of a triumphal arch: in the lower section, the two doors at the sides serve as points of access from the High Sacristy for the clergy; the central arch contains sculptures of *St John the Baptist, St Jerome* and *St Bernard*; in an arcosolium in the second section, above, is a *recumbent statue of Cardinal Mendoza* in pontifical vestments, and above it a relief with the Virgin adored by angels. On the outer face,

Neo-Classical Ionic order architecture of the exterior is the work of Ignacio Haan (1800).

6. The Chapel of San Martín. The screen bears the legend in gold letters on a sky-blue band: "Esta obra hizo maestre Juan Francés, maestre mayor de las rejas" ("This work was made by Master Juan Francés, chief screen-maker"). The Plateresque altarpiece was recomposed in the 16th century with panels (by a number of artists) dating from the second half of the 15th century. The central panel of *St Martin* is ascribed to the Master of Avila, the *Visitation* and *Magdalene* are by the Master of San Ildefonso, and the remainder, generally ascribed to Francisco de Amberes and sometimes to Juan de Borgoña, date from the beginning of the 16th century. In the first section are: the *Birth of the Virgin, St Andrew, St Martin Sharing His Cloak, St James the Less,* and the *Appearance of Christ Risen to Mary Magdalene*. In the second section are: the *Visitation, St James the Great, St Martin, St John, and Mary Magdalene*. The third section contains: *St Thomas Aquinas, St Peter, St Thomas, St Paul and St Thomas of Villanueva*. To each side is a tomb with Plateresque ornamentation and recumbent effigies, again by Vasco de la Zarza's circle: the one on the left is the resting place of Juan López de León, while that on the right is of Tomás González de Villanueva. Together both canons endowed and restored this chapel at the beginning of the 16th century. The chapel also contains two *Virgin and Child* groups and the figure of a saint, all of painted clay and dating from the 16th century. The stained-glass window was made by Enrique Alemán in 1488.

On the pillar in front of this chapel is a small altarpiece of the *Annunciation* (dating from the first third of the 17th century) painted by a follower of El Greco's.

7. The Retrochoir Chapels. Of the various chapels built into the walls surrounding the choir (see p. 28) only the three in the retrochoir still exist. The most interesting is the one on the left known as the Chapel of El Cristo Tendido. Founded in 1510 by Canon Nicolás Ortiz, it has an interesting group of sculptures of the *Descent from the Cross* dating from the early-16th century. Known as the *Virgen de la Estrella*, the chapel in the middle belonged to the Cofradía de Laneros ("Wool Guild"); the Virgin was gilded and painted in 1543 by P. López de Tejeda and the sides were faced with various types of

Screen and pulpits of the Main Chapel, by Francisco de Villalpando (1538-1548). *

marble by Juan Guillén in 1646 on the orders of Archbishop Borja. In 1645 Alonso de Zamora began work on the screen, completing it, like the altar, by the time of Portocarrero. Both bear Portocarrero's coat of arms and Archbishop Valero (d. 1720) is buried in front of the screen. The Chapel of *Santa Catalina*, on the right, contains sculptures of *St Catherine, St Agnes* and *St Lucy,* painted and gilded by Pedro López de Tejeda in 1543.

Until 1791 there were four similar chapels at the sides of the choir but these were covered over with small Neo-Classical marble altarpieces (see p. 30).

8. Chapel of San Eugenio. The screen (c. 1527) is by Domingo de Céspedes. The 13th-century architecture is intact. Made by the Masters Pedro and Oliver, the altarpiece was designed by Enrique Egas and Master Rodrigo in 1500. The statue of St Eugenius was made by Copín in 1517. The panels of scenes from the *Life and Passion of Christ* were painted (c. 1395) by the Florentine Gerardo Starnina for the original altarpiece of the Chapel of La Epifanía; when they were repositioned here they were touched up by Juan de Borgoña. To the right is *the tomb of Fernando Gudiel* (1278), a magnificent Mudéjar piece with elements typical of Almohad influence — an engrailed and stilted arch, a frieze of stalactite-work and interlacing ornamentation, and epigraphic decoration in naskhi characters. To the left is *the Plateresque tomb of Bishop Fernando del Castillo* (1521), whose restoration of the chapel has remained unchanged. This was previously the site of the Parish Church of San Pedro until Archbishop Sancho de Rojas erected the present one (see p. 50). All the chapels we have seen on this side were chosen as mausoleums by rich canons of Toledo around 1500. In the process, old chapels were occupied and redecorated.

9. The large St. Christopher was painted by Gabriel de Rueda in 1638 to replace a picture which had hung there at least since the 15th century. Its size (11 metres in height) is due to the once very widespread belief that whoever saw St Christopher's image would not die in the next three days. Behind it are the old archive of musical scores and a staircase leading up to the Emperor's Organ and the vaults and upper galleries.

opposite the Sacristy, an altar with *St Helena and the Holy Cross* occupies the lower arch, which was originally open so that the Main Chapel would be visible from the ambulatory; in the section above is the *Eternal Father.* Together, the inner and outer faces display the twelve apostles. Within the Main Chapel, where the alterations ordered by Cisneros were again carried out in the Gothic style, the Renaissance tomb of Cisneros's predecessor Mendoza comes as a sharp contrast, particularly if we bear in mind that it was commissioned before the alterations and was completed at about the same time.

Another contrast of styles is to be seen high above: below the windows run Mudéjar galleries with horse-shoe arches resting on coupled colonnettes — the most ancient ornamentation in this area as they date from the 13th century and seem to have been an attempt to

The Descent from the Cross in the Chapel of El Cristo Tendido in the retrochoir.

adapt the style imported from France to Toledo tastes. The arches contain large statues of saints.

The chancel stands three steps higher than the floor of the rest of the building and is paved with red and white marble. It is enclosed by a great screen which, within this area, is the most recent work, as Francisco de Villalpando was awarded the contract for it in 1538, taking ten years to complete it. This is confirmed by a Latin inscription: "Worship the Lord at the entrance to His Tabernacle. First day of April 1548". The most monumental piece of all Spanish Renaissance screen-work, it is divided up into two horizontal and five vertical sections surmounted with the coats of arms of Charles V (with the "Plus Ultra") and those of the Cathedral and Cardinal Silíceo, all originally silvered and gilded. Two superb octagonal *pulpits* displaying exotic pilasters and caryatids, beautiful reliefs, prophets, the Evangelists, and the Silíceo coat of arms, also form part of it. For this masterpiece Villalpando used the bronze of the statue from the tomb of Álvaro de Luna (see p. 36). The pulpits were used for the reading of the lessons from the Gospel (left) and the Epistles (right) at high mass, and for sermons (right).

At the transept, on the last pillar between the two side aisles, are three small altarpieces: two dating from the first half of the 16th century and dedicated to *SS. Jerome and Augustine* and the *Presentation of the Child in the Temple*, while the third is a 17th-century canvas of *St Francesco di Paula* by Ribera's school.

10. The monumental interior face of the doorway known as the **Puerta de los Leones** in the south transept dates from the 15th and 16th centuries and reflects different styles. The Gothic lower section was carved by Juan Alemán around 1460 at the same time as the exterior face (see p. 56) was being made. The central pillar displays an image of the *Saviour* with, above it, on the tympanum, the *Tree of Jesse*,

View of the exterior of the choir with the screen by Francisco de Céspedes (1541-1548).

(Below) St Christopher, by Gabriel de Rueda (1638) on the wall of the south aisle.

culminating in the *Virgin and Child*. The second section is Plateresque and displays the coat of arms of Cardinal Tavera; it was carved in 1540 by a number of artists, including Copín, Aleas, Melchor de Salmerón, Juan de Aguirre, Bernardino Bonifacio, Guillén and Jamete. In the centre is a medallion with the *Coronation of the Virgin* either by Gregorio Pardo or Bigarny, while to the sides are *David and Solomon*, both by Diego Copín. Above this, in the third section, is the *Emperor's Organ*, financed by Charles V; it was played only during processions and when the Te Deum was sung. On the spandrels of the five arches above it are the imperial eagles with the coat of arms of Castile and León. All the Plateresque work was directed by Alonso de Covarrubias. The large rose window displays Cardinal Quiroga's coat of arms.

Each of the two doors is made up of thirty-five panels splendidly carved (1541-42) by Diego and Miguel Copín and other craftsmen, among these Diego de Velasco, who also carved the

The choir

In a privileged position opposite the high altar, this was the area in which the Cathedral clergy sang the liturgical hours. The clergy comprised the archbishop, fourteen canons who were *dignidades,* forty more canons, fifty *racioneros,* fifty choir chaplains, and a third group of canons known as *extravagantes;* in addition to these there were acolytes, choir boys, lectors, cantors and musicians.

To accommodate all these, the superb choir stalls were built and furnished with music-rests, organs and other items for song and prayer.

The choir is separated from the crossing by a grandiose *screen* (1541-1548) designed by Domingo Céspedes which, like Villalpando's,

View of the choir: the lower stalls by Rodrigo Alemán (1489-1495), and the upper stalls by Alonso Berruguete and Felipe Bigarny (1538-1543).

(Right) a scene from the War of Granada on a backrest in the lower choir stalls.

(Below) detail from one of the seats in the lower choir stalls.

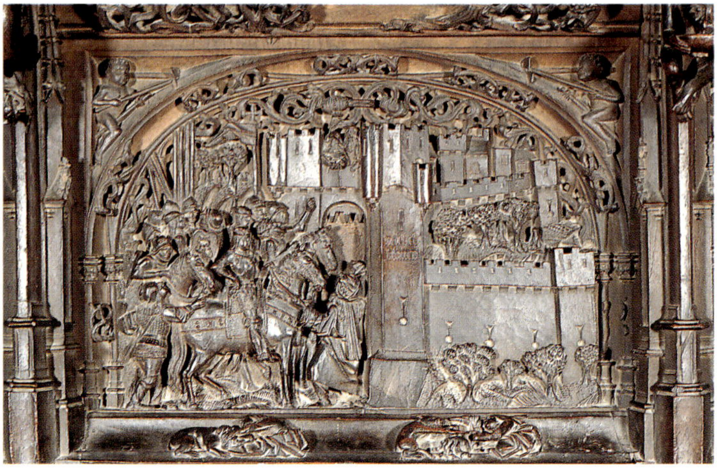

fleurons that serve as studs (1548). On the outside, the doors are covered with superb bronze reliefs made, like the knockers, by Francisco de Villalpando, who received the commission for them in 1551; as Villalpando died before completing them, they were finished (before 1564) by his brother, Rui Díaz del Corral.

To both sides of the door are beautiful funerary arcosolia; like the whole of the first section, they are Gothic and date from the 15th century. On the right-hand side there are no recumbent sculptures, but the back is beautifully decorated with two arches, Gothic tracery and reliefs, and the tomb displays mournful figures under arches. On the left-hand side and within the matching Gothic decoration are a beautiful orant of Canon Alfonso de Rojas (d. 1577) and reliefs of the *Annunciation* and *St Clare*. There is also a fine Plateresque screen.

The pillar on the left of the entrance and next to the *tomb of Alonso de Rojas* displays a small altarpiece of *Abbot St Benedict* by Ramón Bayeu. On the pillar immediately in front of this, above the stoup (made by Doménico Genovés in 1513, and exactly the same as the one on the other side of the transept), is a 16th-century statue of the *Virgin and Child*. To the right of this is the small altarpiece of *St Clare with Don Alonso de Rojas*, dating from the mid-16th century, with a *Saviour* in the attic. On the other side of the

was gold- and silver-plated. Both were completed at the same time, when Charles V was king, Paul III was pope and Silíceo was Archbishop of Toledo.

As early as the 14th century, when the walls separating the choir from the side aisles were built, it had been necessary to install seats, but between 1489 and 1543 these were replaced by the present upper and lower stalls — the most grandiose in Spain — as befitted the wealth of the See and Chapter and the numerous clergy who sang there each day. There were two groups: the *Archbishop's choir*, who sat on the right-hand side (from the high altar), and the *Dean's choir*, on the left.

The *lower choir stalls* were carved by Rodrigo Alemán between 1489 and 1495 and were intended for use by the *extravagantes,* the choir chaplains and Haro chaplains, the salaried singers, who sat in front of lecterns, and for ailing prebendaries who, unwilling or unable to climb stairs, preferred the lower seats. The area contains fifty stalls. On the backrests of each and on four others (in the two corners) are reliefs depicting some episode from the great event then taking place in Castile and one in which Cardinal Mendoza himself (then archbishop) personally had a hand — the conquest of the kingdom of Granada. The seats bear the names of almost all the cities captured. The arms, the stair rails, the misericordes and other parts of the seats are adorned with countless animals and very curious scenes.

The action illustrated on each chair is indicated in the diagram on the back flap.

The lower stalls opposite the entrance are divided in two by five steps. The three seats at the top of these steps were used only by the

The choir. (Left) the Transfiguration, by Berruguete and (right) a detail from the stalls carved by Bigarny. *

Archbishop, the Dean and the Archdeacon of Toledo. In front of these a bench was placed for the *caperos,* that is for the members of the Chapter whose duty it was to lead prayer — between 2 and 6 according to the importance of the feast day — all dressed in chasubles and bearing sceptres. The innermost stairs at the sides were for use by the *dignidades* and the eight oldest canons in each choir; the other stairs were used by the remaining canons and the *racioneros.*

The *upper stalls* were begun forty years later, in 1538. Diego de Siloé, Alonso Berruguete and Felipe Bigarny (Felipe de Borgoña) were invited to submit projects. Berruguete and Bigarny were each awarded half the project, which was completed in 1543, as two Latin inscriptions confirm: the one in the archbishop's choir (right) states the year and the names of the current pope, emperor and archbishop, while that in the Dean's choir (left) bears the legend, "This work, both that of marble and that of wood, was carved on this side by Felipe de Borgoña,

pillar is a 17th-century *Guardian Angel,* a copy of a work by Ramírez.

11. The Chapel of Santa Lucía (now the Chapel of El Sagrado Corazón). To the sides of the entrance arch are small altarpieces with marble frames with stucco medallions above carved by Mariano Salvatierra. On the right are *St Bartholomew* by Maella (1786) and, above, a relief of *SS Thomas of Villanueva and Julian;* on the left is a commemorative inscription where Caravaggio's *St John* (now in the sacristy) once hung, with a relief of *SS. Justus and Pastor* above it.

The simple screen dates from the 16th century. Inside the chapel there is a late-18th

The Descent, by Gregorio Pardo, on the backrest of the Archbishop's stall in the choir.

century Neo-Classical altarpiece — in the place where Agustín Navarro's painting of *St Lucy* (now in the Antechapel of the Sacrarium) once hung. On the side walls are Baroque paintings of *St Peter Martyr* and *St Peter Arbués*. The remains of several members of the Palomeque family were transferred to this chapel from the Chapel of Reyes Viejos in 1498.

Between this chapel and that of Reyes Viejos is a small altarpiece of the *Virgin of Guadalupe* (1657).

12. The Chapel of Reyes Viejos. The inscription in Gothic script on the right-hand wall sums up the history of this chapel: "Esta capilla del Rey don Sancho de gloriosa memoria fue fundada so invocación de la cruz do está ahora el altar mayor de esta Santa Iglesia, y quedando los cuerpos de los Reyes a los lados del altar fue trasladada aquí por mandado de los católicos Príncipes Don Fernando y Doña Isabel NN.SS., en 18 de enero de 1498 años" ("This chapel of King Don Sancho, whose memory is glorious, was founded on the invocation of the cross where the high altar of this Holy Church now stands, and, with the bodies of the Kings

and on the opposite side by the Spaniard Berruguete. As the creativeness of the artificers competed so will the opinions of those who examine this work always compete". As far as 19th- and 20th-century tastes are concerned, the "tie" between the two artists was a clear victory for Berruguete.

The very abundant iconography of the choir stalls is indicated in the diagram on the back flap.

The contract signed by the two sculptors and the Chapter (formalized on 1st January 1539), stipulated that: each was to make 35 stalls, including the alabaster reliefs in the upper section; the archbishop's chair was to be made by Bigarny; and that all would be completed within three years. But Bigarny died on 10th November 1543, while he was finishing his stalls and carving the altarpiece of the Descent (at the foot of which he is buried, see p. 11). As he was not able to carve the archbishop's chair, Berruguete did so, although the alabaster relief with the Descent is actually by Gregorio Pardo (1548). As with the stalls, the reliefs on the backrests are of walnut and depict saints. Each bears Cardinal Tavera's coat of arms except for the archbishop's seat, which displays the coat of arms of Tavera's successor, Silíceo.

Each seat is framed by a semi-circular arch resting on slender marble columns, adding richness and spatial grace to the stalls as a whole. Above the seats, in the attic, alabaster reliefs depict sixty-eight patriarchs from the Old Testament; at the end of each choir and closest to the screen is Cardinal Tavera's coat of arms.

Berruguete made the Archbishop's chair in Valladolid and came to Toledo in 1545 to position it; he then carved the superb group of figures above it and the two adjacent seats in Cogolludo alabaster. This group contains the *Transfiguration of Christ*, with the figures of Moses, Elijah, and the apostles Peter, John and James, and is surmounted with a small open temple of gilded iron with highly imaginative columns. Also by Berruguete are the bronze columns supporting the vault over the archbishop's chair, which is higher than the others. The whole of the choir stalls, particularly the section made by Berruguete, is considered a major work of Spanish Renaissance art.

The same can be said of the two large cast-iron and gilded bronze lecterns on each side of the choir, although they are somewhat later — 1570. They supported the large books from which the canonical hours were sung and were made by the Nicolás de Vergaras, father and son. Nicolás the Elder (1517-1574), son of the glazier Arnao de Vergara, was the Cathedral's master glazier and sculptor from 1542. His son, the sculptor Nicolás de Vergara the Younger (1542- c. 1606), learned from and worked under him, and on his father's death inherited his post at the Cathedral as well as a number of his projects. He was appointed

(Left) detail from one of the lecterns in the choir, by Vergara (1570). *

The Virgen Blanca or "White Virgin", to whom the Prime Altar in the choir is dedicated.

remaining at the sides of the altar, was transferred here upon the orders of the catholic Princes, our Lords Don Ferdinand and Doña Isabella, on the 18th day of January in the year 1498"). This transfer took place as the result of Cisneros's decision to extend the presbytery (see p. 14) at the cost of the old Chapel of Reyes Viejos; the royal tombs remained at the sides of the high altar but thereafter the funeral rites

master builder in 1587. Nicolás the Elder was the most important figure in Toledo Mannerist classicism and one of the most outstanding proponents of 16th-century Spanish architecture.

The lecterns consist of three Doric columns supporting an entablature depicting: on the archbishop's side of the choir (right), *David Persecuted by Saul,* and a *Passage from the Apocalypse*; and, on the Dean's side (left), the *Bearing of the Ark of the Covenant*, and the *Crossing of the Red Sea.*

In the centre of the choir is the *Lectern of the Eagle*, used for the reading of various prayers said during the services. It is entirely of bronze and dates from two periods. The hexagonal, castle-shaped pedestal, of openwork and with an iron frame inside, displays sculptures representing the twelve apostles, six archbishops of Toledo and doctors of the Church. It is German and was made around 1425, although Vicente Salinas added the Eagle in 1646. There were three other portable lecterns, one dating from 1517 and made by one of the carvers who worked with Petit Jean on the altarpiece, while the other two were Plateresque and were made by Diego de Velasco in 1558. The songbooks contain a number of fine miniatures, but more beautiful still are the books used up until the time when Toledo prayer was forbidden at the end of the 16th century; these are now in the Chapter House Library.

Next to the screen is the *Prime Altar*, so called because mass was said at it after the canonical hour of matins. Its beautiful balustrade, commissioned at the same time as the bronze work of the Puerta de los Leones in 1551 (see p. 26) is by Francisco de Villalpando, although it was completed by Villalpando's brother Rui Díaz del Corral in 1564.

The retrochoir: St Agatha, a Plateresque wood-carving in the Chapel of Santa Catalina.

(said by thirteen chaplains) took place in the Chapel of **El Espíritu Santo,** which had been founded around 1290 by Archbishop Gonzalo Díaz Palomeque.

Cisneros could not have ordered the decoration of the chapel, for it is Plateresque and dates from the time of Fonseca, as the latter's coat of arms on Domingo de Céspedes's magnificent screen (1529) proves. On the left, the three altarpieces were made by Francisco Comontes (1539): the one in the centre surmounted by the Holy Cross (a reference to the dedication of the old Chapel of Reyes Viejos) is of Hispano-Flemish panels of joyous and glorious scenes from the Life of Christ by Juan Alfón (1418). Also by Alfón are the panels of the small altarpieces — of *St John the Evangelist* and *St Catherine*. The 16th-century slate frontals retain vestiges of their original colours. A beautiful Gothic doorway with a herald above leads to the sacristy and the royal chapel archives.

To the right is the area which once served as the choir for the thirteen chaplains, although the stalls no longer exist. The Plateresque screen was made in the workshops of Céspedes (1558). The

Above this altar is the French-style Gothic *Virgen Blanca* or "White Virgin", dating from the 14th century.

The marble floor dates from 1539, the previous one being of gravestones, including those of Archbishops Gómez Manrique, Gonzalo de Aguilar and Blas Fernández de Toledo. Only a few inscriptions on the flags remind us that these Archbishops are buried here, for although new effigies were planned for them, they were never made.

Above the choir and at the sides are a number of galleries for the organists. Here there are two large organs. On the right, the organ of the archbishop's choir was made (1755-1756) by Pedro Liborna Echevarría. The Baroque case (1757) is by Germán López and was gilded by Prospero Mortola. The organ on the Dean's side was made (1796-1797) by José Berdalonga. Its 6,000 pipes are well arranged in a Neo-Classical Corinthian case designed, apparently, by Ignacio Haan, who took his inspiration from those at El Escorial. It was built by Juan Hernández and the sculptures were made by Mariano Salvatierra.

A small organ was sometimes used during matins. The altar bells were played during the elevation at sung mass, the Te Deum and solemn Gloriae, etc.

On the first pillar, next to the Baroque organ, is an orant of Diego López de Haro, Lord of Vizcaya; a distinguished warrior at the Battle of Las Navas de Tolosa, it was he who shared out the booty. López de Haro financed the whole of the side nave from his statue to the Puerta de los Escribanos and made donations to the Chapter, who showed their gratitude by raising this statue to him as an example of the model Christian knight.

THE AREA AROUND THE MAIN CHAPEL AND THE CHOIR

Before leaving the Main Chapel and choir a walk around their enclosing walls is well worthwhile as they were built to mark the air of solemnity and privilege inherent in these areas dedicated to worship.

THE RETROCHOIR

The Retrochoir was erected by Archbishop Tenorio in the 14th century. Originally it had sixty-seven red marble columns over three metres tall which, apparently, came from the extension of the old mosque in the 10th century. However, as the capitals that have remained in their original positions prove, fifteen were removed to make space for the entrances to the choir (with screens by Juan Corbella, 1561), the retrochoir chapels (see p. 20) and for enlarging the chapels which once stood where the small Neo-Classical altarpieces now are.

The retrochoir, with the Chapels of El Cristo Tendido, La Estrella and Santa Catalina.

organ dates from the late-17th century. The chapel also contains a 16th-century painted wooden candelabrum. The Virgin of El Alcázar dates from the beginning of this century.

13. The Chapel of El Santo Sepulcro is beneath the presbytery of the Main Chapel (see p.p. 12, 14) and is formed by five vaults, two at the sides (with staircases) and three in the middle (with altars). On the central altar is a sculpture of the *Entombment* carved by Copín (1514) and painted by Juan de Borgoña. On the altar to its left are a wood-carving of *St Julian* and panels of *St Simon* and *St John* painted by a pupil of Gerardo Starnina's at the end of the 14th century. The altar on the right displays a *Stigmata of St Francis;* dating from the first half of the 17th century, it was painted by Francisco Fernández, a Toledo artist. The two canvases at the sides of these came from Madrid and are dated 1663. They are: the *Slaughter of the Innocents* by Francisco Rizi and *St John the Baptist*, either by Rizi or J. A. Escalante. **The retrochoir behind the high altar** (on this page) was executed by Juan Guas in the second half of the 15th century.

14. The Chapel of Santa Ana is a fine Plateresque work financed by Canon Juan de Mariana between 1560 and 1565. The screen was wrought by Benito de la Capilla. The altarpiece contains a sculpture of *St Anne*, various panels of the *Evangelists,* and a *Baptism of Christ* in the attic. On the left is the tomb of the chapel's patron with an orant.

The small altarpiece with the *Nativity, Calvary* and the *Virgin and Child* on the pillar in front of the chapel dates from the first half of the 16th century.

15. The Chapel of San Juan Bautista. The Gothic screen surmounted with thistles dates from the 15th century, as do the beautiful tracery forming the chapel's inner face, the pinnacles above the altarpiece, and the tomb, on the left, of Archdeacon Fernando Díaz de Toledo (d. 1452). Above the tomb is a triptych on board with the *Descent*. Made of wood and of the Corinthian order, the altarpiece dates from the first half of the 17th century and was financed by the *racionero* Gabriel Pérez Cerro (d. 1641). In 1790, however, part of the woodwork was removed and what remained was painted to imitate marble. It also displays a sculpture of *St John the Baptist* and pictures of *St Jerome* and *St Francis of Assisi*.

The sacristy of this chapel was once the old

The second section in this area contains scenes from the Old Testament — from the Creation to the Tables of the Law — and were also carved when Tenorio was archbishop. Of these, 56 medallions remain, for when the upper choir stalls and the group of figures in Berruguete's *Transfiguration* were made, the upper part of the retrochoir was renovated with two reliefs by Nicolás de Vergara the Elder. These were *Innocence* (which stands naked with a lamb) next to Adam and Eve (still in the Garden of Eden), and *Guilt,* (clothed and with a skull at her feet).

The four small Neo-Classical altarpieces mentioned above are of marble and have fluted Ionic pilasters with gilded bronze bases and capitals. They were carved by Martín Marichalar and Daniel Idrac in 1791. The statues were made by Mariano Salvatierra, with *St Stephen* and *St Michael* opposite the Chapel of San Pedro, and *St Mary Magdalene* and *St Elizabeth of Hungary* opposite the Chapel of San Eugenio.

The area behind the high altar

The ambulatory runs around the first, semi-circular, section of the nave. As we have seen (p. 14), after the alterations made by Cisneros this formed part of the Main Chapel but it originally contained (13th century) a Royal Chapel standing on two levels — a curious arrangement which would seem to be explained by an attempt to establish a comparison between the Primate See of Spain and the Temple of Jerusalem and by extension between the King of Castile and King Solomon. In the Middle Ages the idea of the Temple of Solomon was that of a structure situated within the rectangular walls of Jerusalem and this is how it is depicted in idealised representations of the Holy City and in others of the "Celestial City" or New Jerusalem. To this mystical parallel between Toledo Cathedral, the Holy City and the New Jerusalem, were dedicated the two floors of the central area of the ambulatory, arranged in the same way as in many other churches of the Order of the Knights Templar, with the lower part dedicated to the *Holy Sepulchre* and the upper to the Holy Cross.

The area behind the high altar, i.e. the five façades facing the ambulatory from this "semi-cylindrical" centre of the Cathedral, was decorated in the second half of the 15th century by order of Mendoza, whose title was "Cardinal of the Holy Cross" and who placed all his zeal in the "crusade" against the Kingdom of Granada. It is therefore not surprising that he should have wished the exterior of the "Royal Chapel of the Holy Cross" to be especially important. The work was assigned to two architects: Juan Guas was entrusted with the two south sections, while Martín Sánchez Bonifacio was commissioned to do the north sections. Both, however, followed the same plan — which

*Detail from the Santa Lucía wall enclosing the Main Chapel on its south side.**

corresponds to the continuation of the *side screens* of the Main Chapel (see p.p. 18-19) — but with some modernisation.

In the areas closest to the crossing, the first section is divided up by a point of access to the Chapel of El Sepulcro and a number of spaces affording a view of the Main Chapel. The impost between the two displays the coat of arms of Cardinal Mendoza with the Cross of

Chapel of San Bricio and has a late 15th-century Gothic altarpiece.

16. The Chapel of San Gil. Although the 13th-century architecture of this chapel is intact, the noteworthy decoration is Mannerist (1573) and was commissioned by Canon Miguel Díaz (d. 1573). Díaz stipulated that in this chapel alone 1,196 masses were to be celebrated each year. The screen was made by Benito de la Capilla. Above the marble altarpiece are two columns, one Doric, the other Ionic, and there are also alabaster reliefs of *St Gil*, *The Evangelists*, *St Michael*, the *Conception* and *The Eternal Father*. The pictorial decoration with grotesques on the vault is ascribed to Nicolás de Vergara the Elder, who may also have supervised the whole of the work in the chapel.

On the pillar in front of the chapel, the small altarpiece of the Pietà dates from the first half of the 16th century.

17. The Entrance to the Chapter House dates from the beginning of the 16th century and cuts diagonally across the original 13th-century apse. This was once the Chapel of Santa Isabel de Hungría (Elizabeth's image is depicted in the stained-glass window) built by a certain Cebrián, whose tomb is on the right-hand side. In the centre is the magnificent Gothic doorway of the **Antechamber to the Chapter House** (see p. 35), designed by Diego Copín (1500) and carved by Antonio Gutiérrez. Above the ogee arch are Gothic thistles (between the two gilded pinnacles) and statues, carved by Copín, of the *Virgin*, *St John the Evangelist* and *St James the Great*.

18. The Chapel of San Nicolás. The floor of this chapel is higher because around 1535 a doorway to a courtyard and several adjacent rooms dating from the time of Mendoza was made here. It was also at that time that the beautiful doorway in the lower section was carved; it was decorated with Tavera's coat of arms and typical Plateresque ornamentation — masks, cornucopias, nude torsos, heads, children, etc. In the upper part are a late-15th century screen and a 17th-century altarpiece (with 15th-century panels) depicting *St Peter*, *St Paul* and *St Nicholas of Bari*. There has been no altar here since 1790, as it was moved to the Chapel of Santiago and a chest of drawers for the uniforms of the *seises* was put in its place.

Detail from the coffered ceiling in the Chapter House, by Diego López de Arenas and Francisco Lara.

19. The Chapel of La Trinidad. The ground plan of this chapel is intact but its stellar vault with gilded pendants dates from the end of the 15th century and is higher than the original one. It was endowed and decorated by Canon Gutiérre Díaz (d. 1522) in the Plateresque style. The screen was wrought by Juan Piñas in 1520. The altarpiece is after Comontes's circle and the predella depicts the *Four Doctors of the Church* and the *Entombment*. The first section contains the *Embrace Before the Golden Gate*, the *Saviour* and the *Birth of the Virgin*, the second section the *Annunciation*, the *Assumption* and the *Nativity*, while at the top are a *Calvary* and various saints painted on panels in the intercolumniation. On the left is a recumbent effigy of Canon Gutierre Díaz, who endowed and decorated the chapel, as an inscription opposite it states.

20. The Chapel of San Ildefonso. This grandiose funeral construction raised to Cardinal Archbishop Gil Carrillo de Albornoz replaced the old central chapel of the apse and the two smaller adjacent ones. The central chapel was dedicated to St Ildefons at the time of the Cathedral's foundation in 1215 by Archbishop Rodrigo Jiménez de Rada, who instituted the *Mass of the Saint*. The glorification of the Toledo bishop and saint reaches its highest point in this climax of the east end (opposite the great doorway) which also depicts the miracle of the Descent of the Virgin to reward the saint with a chasuble.

As his burial chapel Albornoz (d. 1367), a minister of Alfonso XI's and the founder of the Spanish college in Bologna, built a masterpiece of Spanish Gothic architecture of the second half of the 14th century. Due to both its shape and position in the Cathedral's east end, this octagonal burial chapel proved to be the precursor of other large chapels to appear throughout the 15th century beginning with that of Santiago immediately next to it. The high groined vault with gilded lobes on the ribs and Albornoz's coat of arms was illuminated with large windows (now mainly walled up); the remaining windows display the coats of arms of Silíceo and Quiroga. The chapel's original sculptural decoration was limited to four reliefs on the walls of the diagonals, one of which is now lost; the remaining three depict the *Tetramorph*, the *Coronation of the Virgin* and the *Last Judgement*. In the centre of the chapel, resting on six lions, is the foun-

Jerusalem and its four equal branches. The second section contains 16 medallions with scenes from the Life of Christ, beginning with the Annunciation and ending with the Transfiguration. The third section contains statues of saints and kings surmounted with crenellation. The two façades of the area behind the high altar and nearest to the middle of the ambulatory were somewhat defaced in the 18th century, when the *Transparente*, occupying the central section behind the high altar, was built.

The Transparente

This is not only a major work of Spanish Baroque but also an extremely noteworthy example of European late-Baroque. It is an extremely rich altarpiece of bronze and various types of Spanish marble (except for the statues of Genoese marble), depicting the apotheosis of the Blessed Sacrament of the Eucharist, and was built with the excuse of illuminating the sacrarium of the high altar by means of a central oval window with a bronze grille forming rays of light. To this end, an opening was made in the vault of the ambulatory in such a way that the glory of God appears to be shining through. Everything — the plans, the painting, even the silver lamp hanging in front of it — is the work of Narciso Tomé, and it was solemnly inaugurated in June 1732. Two years later, Archbishop Diego de Astorga y Céspedes, who had erected it and is buried in front of it, died. The first section contains the Virgin and Child and reliefs of *David and Ahimelec* and the Meeting of *Abigail and David*; it also bears the signature in Latin of "Narciso Tomé, master of architects of this Holy Primate Church, [who] designed, sculpted and

The Transparente (1732). Complete view and a detail of the vault. It was designed and painted by Narciso Tomé, who also carved the sculptures.

painted all this work that is composed of marble, jasper and bronze". The second section contains statues of *St Leocadia* (left) and *St Casilda* (right), with the *Last Supper* above. Higher still and to the sides are *St Eugenius* and *St Ildefons,* while surmounting it all are *The Three Theological Virtues* — Faith, Hope and Charity. Even when Tomé drew his first sketches, he intended to include these last five statues (of Carrara marble) in the Transparente. Brought to Toledo in 1677, they were, in fact, works executed previously by an anonymous Genoese sculptor

der's tomb, dating from the second half of the 14th century. The recumbent Cardinal is in pontifical dress and the ark is adorned with the figures of saints and hooded mourners beneath twenty-two pointed arches with Gothic canopies and pinnacles resting on colonnettes.

In the walls of the chapel are the tombs of other important persons related in some way to the Cardinal. On the left are those of: the nuncio Alejandro Frumento (d. 1580), and Archbishop Juan Martínez de Contreras (d. 1434); and on the right, next to the altarpiece, is the superb *tomb of Alonso Carrillo de Albornoz* by Vasco de la Zarza, a masterpiece of Spanish Plateresque art (1515, gilded in 1545). At its side is the tomb of his brother, Íñigo López Carrillo de Mendoza, viceroy of Sardinia, displaying a recumbent statue. Next to the screen and with no indication is the *tomb of Cardinal de Borja* (d. 1645).

The old 15th-century Gothic altarpiece, by Rodrigo Alemán, the image maker Juan de Bruselas and the painters Andrés Segura and Villoldo, was replaced in 1780 by the present one — a reflection of the courtly magnificence

Chapel of San Ildefonso. The Neo-Classical altarpiece by Ventura Rodríguez and Manuel Alvarez.

of Charles III and Cardinal Lorenzana. Designed by Ventura Rodríguez, it is made of various materials: the bronze-work was by Miguel Jiménez, while the marble came from Garciatum and other Spanish quarries, and from Carrara for the sculptures. The high relief for the *Descent* was executed by Manuel Alvarez, while the angels on the fronton and the busts of *St Leander* and *St Isidore* over the small doors at the side were carved by Juan Pascual de Mena. This Neo-Classical contrast to the *Transparente,* which it faces (see p. 32), was inaugurated on 22nd May 1783. On the left is an altarpiece with *St Nicholas of Tolentino* (1646) with a *Christ of the Cross* at its side in which the position of the cross is almost opposite to that traditionally portrayed. It is a curious fact that this image was sent to Spain from Italy accompanying the body of Cardinal Albornoz and that it was decreed that whoever helped with its transfer would automatically receive indulgences from the Pope. During restoration in the 19th century it was badly repainted. The screens were made by Master Pablo (1484). On the pillars forming the three openings into the Chapel of San Ildefonso are three small altarpieces: those of the *Last Supper* and *St Gregory* are of gilded wood and date from the 16th century, while the Gothic *Virgin and Child*, which stands on a Visigothic capital, is of painted stone and dates from the 14th century. On the pillars of the ambulatory facing this chapel away from the Transparente are two small altarpieces: the marble one on the right displays reliefs of *SS. Vincent, Sabina and Cristeta*, is Baroque and dates from the 18th century; that on the left, by Mariano Salvatierra (1790), is Neo-Classical, of stucco, and depicts *SS. Cosme and Damian.* On the vault of the ambulatory, just above the entrance to the Chapel of San Ildefonso, is a portrait of *Esteban Illán* on horseback. It is a copy, by Narciso Tomé, of the original 13th-century portrait on the vault which was destroyed when the *Transparente* was built. Illán was a prominent citizen and procurator of Toledo in the 13th century who succeeded in obtaining the extension of the fiscal privileges originally granted to the city by Alfonso VIII.

21. The Chapel of Santiago occupies the site of three of the Cathedral's original chapels, one small and two large (one of these dedicated to commissioned by Cardinal Pascual de Aragón. The cardinal, wishing to build a Transparente himself, had paid the painter Francisco Rizi for plans in 1672. As the statues were thus intended to be viewed from closer quarters, their high position does not allow their beauty to be fully appreciated, especially in the case of the Virtues. Cardinal Portocarrero continued gathering materials: except for the statues made in Genoa, the whole group is made of Spanish marble — from Cabra, Montesclaros, Urda, Estremoz, Granada, Tortosa, San Pablo, Saelices and Torrubia, among other places.

Tomé broke open the central section of the vault over the ambulatory to illuminate the Transparente and decorated the walls of the new dome with statues of angels in an explosion of glory with frescoes illustrating the Eucharist, Benjamin in prison, passages from Gideon, and St John's Vision of the Apocalypse with the 24 elders adoring the Lamb.

View of the Chapter House, with paintings by Juan de Borgoña.

THE LARGE ADJACENT ROOMS

THE CHAPTER HOUSE

When Cardinal Cisneros founded the Capilla Mozárabe ("Mozarabic Chapel", previously the Chapter House, see p. 14), it became necessary to finance the construction of a new room for the Chapter's assemblies. This was carried out between 1504 and 1512 (mainly between 1508 and 1510) by the Cathedral's master builder Enrique Egas in collaboration with the archbishop's architect, Pedro Gumiel.

To reach it, it is necessary to cross the old Chapel of Santa Isabel de Hungría (see p. 32) from the ambulatory through an entrance carved by Copín which leads to the **Chapter House Antechamber**, whose inner area displays beautiful Plateresque decoration and Cisneros's coat of arms. As this room was also used as an archive for the Chapter's minutes, *cabinets* — with beautiful Plateresque reliefs on the pilasters and door

St Thomas à Becket). The tycoon who decided (c. 1435) not only to emulate Cardinal Albornoz de Carrillo but to better him with this great family funeral Chapel was Don Alvaro de Luna, the omnipotent minister and favourite of John II, who was to fall from favour and die on the block in 1453. His widow, Countess Juana Pimentel, and his daughter, María de Luna, second Duchess of El Infantado, ensured that the work was completed. Begun at some time between 1435 and 1440 by Hanequín de Bruselas in the pure Flamboyant Gothic style, it has a profusion of gables and lancet arches in the tradition of the finest Toledo Gothic of the second half of the 15th century. Particularly interesting is the

The Chapel of Santiago with the tombs of its founders, Don Alvaro de Luna and his wife Doña Juana Pimentel.

tracery on the walls separating the chapel from the ambulatory with simple screens. The ceiling is formed by a beautiful stellar vault that is well lit by eight large openings and a window. Above the altarpiece is a large coloured relief of *St James at Clavijo*, while other wall panels depict angels with the coats of arms of the houses of Luna and Pimentel (escallops).

In the centre of the chapel are the *tombs of Don Alvaro de Luna and his wife Doña Juana Pimentel* (1498), ascribed to Pablo Ortíz and Sebastián de Almonacid. Don Alvaro's tomb, with knights of the Order of Santiago kneeling at each corner, is the one on the right; the orant figures at the corners of Doña Juana's tomb are of Franciscan friars.

Other family *tombs* are in wall niches with gables above. To the left of the entrance, they belong to: Archbishop Juan de Cerezuela (d. 1442); Archbishop Pedro de Luna (d. 1404); and Juan de Luna, son of the High Constable. They have recumbent statues ascribed to Ortiz. There is no effigy on the tomb of Don Alvaro's father (on the right, next to the screen), but above is the tomb and effigy of Cardinal Bonel y Orbe (d. 1857).

panels — were built. However, only the cabinet on the left dates from the 16th century, having been commissioned by Cardinal Silíceo (whose coat of arms it displays) and built by Gregorio Pardo between 1549 and 1551. A faithful reproduction of the first, the cabinet on the right was built by Gregorio López in 1780; only the Bourbon coat of arms betrays its 18th-century origin. The decorative mural pictures above of trees and vases with plants and flowers were designed by Juan de Borgoña in 1511 and painted by Luis Medina, Diego López and Alonso Sánchez.

The wooden ceiling in the anteroom was built by Francisco Lara. Mudéjar-style like the portal, it displays stuccowork decoration by Master Pablo and the sculptor Blandino Bonifacio; it was painted and gilded by Arévalo and Alonso Sánchez. Here the diamond-pattern designs and stylised geometric and vegetal decoration so typical of the Mudéjar style all combine with circular Renaissance forms. This mixture of late Flamboyant Gothic and Mudéjar elements together with hints of the forthcoming Renaissance style have come to be known as the *Cisneros style* — classic examples being this room and the chapel of the Colegio Mayor de San Ildefonso in Alcalá de Henares founded by Cardinal Cisneros (and also his burial place).

The door panels were designed (1552) by Master Marcos and carved by Bonifacio.

In the grandiose **Chapter House**, however, it is the Plateresque style which predominates, Mudéjar components having by now disappeared, except in the general shape of the wooden ceiling. Carved in the Renaissance style, it is divided up into coffers containing Cisneros's coat of

arms and emblems of the Virgin. It was designed and begun by Diego López de Arenas and completed by Francisco Lara.

The magnificent *murals* (1508) are by Juan de Borgoña. They depict thirteen scenes from the life of the Virgin and the Passion of Christ divided up by columns in such a way that the wall appears to be a flat open gallery affording an open-air view of: the *Conception of the Virgin* (The Embrace Before the Golden Gate), the *Birth of the Virgin,* the *Presentation in the Temple,* the *Annunciation,* the *Visitation,* the *Circumcision of Christ,* the *Dormition,* the *Assumption,* the *Bestowal of the Chasuble on St Ildefons,* the *Descent from the Cross,* the *Pietà,* the *Resurrection of Christ* and the *Last Judgement.* The *Assumption* was restored by Blas de Prado in 1586 and all thirteen scenes were restored in 1646 by Francisco de Aguirre.

From a historical point of view, **the series of portraits of the Archbishops of Toledo** which runs like a frieze below the Gospel scenes is

(Left) Christ the Judge, a fresco by Juan de Borgoña.

(Right) Detail from the Plateresque wood-carving on one of the cabinets in the Chapter House Anteroom, by Gregorio Pardo.

Commissioned by Doña María de Luna, the Gothic altarpiece of gilded wood was designed by Pedro Gumiel and the sculptures were executed by Juan de Segovia (1488). It also displays a number of magnificent Hispano-Flemish panel paintings: by the de Luna's painter Juan de Segovia are the five panels of the predella, depicting the *Descent* and, at the sides, *the portraits of the founding couple kneeling before SS. Francis and Antony;* the painting above the central

The Birth of the Virgin, a fresco by Juan de Borgoña in the Chapter House.

section is undoubtedly also by Juan de Segovia. Sancho de Zamora, the master of the Chapel of San Ildefonso, painted the eight panels with saints at the sides.

On Gothic corbels in each of the eight corners are sculptures of saints. Beginning on the left of the screen they are: *Nicholas of Bari, Abbot Antony, Francis of Assisi* and *Peter Nolasco; Philip Neri, Barbara, Lawrence* and *Bernard*. Carved by Mariano Salvatierra, they were positioned in the chapel in 1791, when their respective altarpieces on the pillars in the nave and side aisles were removed; on each saint's feast day a portable altar was set up before them to celebrate mass.

This chapel continues to be patronised by the Dukes of El Infantado and at the beginning of this century the family built a new crypt beneath the chapel; it is illuminated by glass panels in the floor. At this time also, the Baroque altars of *St Teresa* (see p. 51) and *St Francis of Borja* (whose image is in the crypt) were removed.

22. The Chapel of Reyes Nuevos. The Chapel of Reyes Nuevos (lit. "New Kings") is the pantheon of the Trastámaras. Its name differentiates it from the Chapel of "Reyes Viejos" ("Old Kings", see p.p. 14, 26). In 1374 Henry II decided to found this funeral chapel for his line, erecting it at the west end of the Cathedral between the tower and the pillar of the Descent (see p. 8). The Chapter and Cardinal Fonseca intended to leave those two sections of the side aisle free for this purpose, but it was not until 1530 that it was decided to build a new chapel on the only site available — a courtyard where the Cathedral's ironwork shops had been situated — as its irregular shape posed problems finally solved, it seems, by the architects Enrique Egas, Diego de Siloé and Alonso de Covarrubias. Covarrubias submitted the project to the Emperor Charles V in 1531 and subsequently built the chapel, completing it in 1534. However, the structure is so Gothic that it seems much more the work of Egas than of Covarrubias. Only the decoration can be said to be typical of the latter, whose first major work in the Cathedral was in fact this fanciful blend of Gothic and Plateresque architectural and decorative systems. Prominent among those who worked on it were the quantity surveyor Alvaro de Monegro, the sculptors and carvers Diego Egas, Melchor de Salmerón, Pedro de Santiesteban, Bernardino Bonifacio,

very interesting. As the patronage of the prelates was essential for the construction and adornment of the Cathedral, it is well worthwhile paying close attention to the faces, the order in which they appear, and the dates of the different pontificates. Below we list the most important ones both from the historical and artistic point of view, indicating the pages on which their main contribution to the Cathedral is discussed, and, whenever possible, the name of the artist who painted the portrait.

The first thirty-two prelates were painted by Juan de Borgoña and occupy all of the area between the Gospel scenes and the seats. They begin with St Eugenius, the first on the left of the archbishop's chair, and circle the room to end with Cisneros, who seems to be looking at the archbishop's chair to his left and challenging his successors in the row below.

The portraits of the earliest prelates in Borgoña's pictures are clearly imaginary, but those painted from the 13th century on display the true likeness, coming from previous portraits and thus the faces of Mendoza and Cisneros are taken from life. Particularly important are the portraits of: Rodrigo Jiménez de Rada (see p. 8); Gil Carrillo de Albornoz (see p. 22); Gómez Manrique (see p. 28); Pedro Tenorio (see p.p. 12, 53); Sancho de Rojas (see p. 52); Juan de Cerezuela (see p.p. 12, 54); Alonso Carrillo; Pedro González de Mendoza (see p.p. 19, 24); and Cisneros (see p. 14, 54).

The series from the time of Cisneros's successor to the present day continues in a very interesting sequence on the backrests of the seats. They depict: Guillermo de Croy (1522) and Alonso de Fonseca

Portraits of Cardinals Mendoza and Cisneros by Juan de Borgoña.

(1526), by Juan de Borgoña; Juan Pardo de Tavera (see p.p. 10, 26) and Juan Martínez Silíceo (see p.p. 22, 24, 26, 36), both by Francisco Comontes; Bartolomé de Carranza (see p. 10), by Luis de Carvajal; Quiroga (see p.p. 43, 50), by Luis de Velasco; the Infante Cardinal Don Alberto, by Cristóbal de Velasco; Loaisa, by Luis de Velasco; Sandoval and Rojas (see p.p. 43 ff.), by Tristán (1610); the Infante Cardinal Don Fernando, by Francisco de Aguirre; Borja, based on a composition by Velázquez (the drawing for which is in the Academia de San Fernando, in Madrid), and a copy originally on his grave and now in the Vestry (see p.p. 34, 46); Moscoso (see p.12), by Rizi (1666); Portocarrero (see p. 44); Astorga (see p. 32); the Infante Cardinal Don Luis de Borbón (see p. 51); Luis Fernández de Córdoba (thought to be by Goya); Lorenzana and Luis María de Borbón (see p. 45), by Esteve; and Inguanzo, by Vicente López.

The Plateresque *Archbishop's Chair* was carved (1509-1514) by Copín, while the wooden benches, which also serve as chests, were made by Francisco Lara (1512) and their edges painted by Luis Medina.

Francisco de Ciudad and Alonso de Talavera, and the gilder Pedro López de Tejeda.

The site made it necessary to create a succession of areas: a rectangular entrance, a trapezoidal vestibule, and the chapel, divided into two four-sided areas separated by one of the buttresses in the Chapel of the De Lunas. Behind this chapel are the sacristy and Chapter House with their very rich and abundant ornamentation, and above it is the Archive.

The lovely **Plateresque doorway**, its columns completely covered with grotesques, is adorned with reliefs and flanked by two statues of Kings of Arms bearing maces and dressed in dalmatics adorned with the *royal coat of arms*, all in coloured and gilded stone. Two macebearers like these, with damask robes and embroidered velvet dalmatics, also stood at each

*View of the Chapel of Reyes Nuevos, designed by Alonso de Covarrubias (1531-1534), paintings by Maella.**

side of the choir of this chapel during services and ceremonies. The entrance, with a cannon vault and octagonal coffers above, occupies the former position of the Chapel of Santa Bárbara; there is a royal coat of arms between the semicircular arch and the old pointed one.

The iron screen is Plateresque and, like all those in this chapel, was made in 1532 by Domingo de Céspedes.

The ceiling above the vestibule is a 17th-century domical vault with a lantern. In the left-hand wall is a large walled-up window with Gothic tracery dating from the end of the 15th century. A display cabinet contains the armour of

THE SACRISTY AND ITS MUSEUMS

Of the large number of rooms which contained the liturgical vestments and ornaments and were used by the officiants before services, some around the Sacristy are now open to the public. Here it should be remembered that in addition to the clergy who sat in the choir, the Cathedral's ecclesiastic and lay staff together numbered six hundred, which included the almost two hundred chaplains and sacristans of the chapels and the one hundred and fifty workmen employed by the Chapter and the Cathedral's building and maintenance department.

The paintings in the **Antesacristy** include: *St Andrew* and *St Peter* crucified, by Vicente Carducho (on either side of the entrance to the Sacristy); opposite, a large *Annunciation,* by Francisco Rizi; *Samson and the Lion*, by José del Castillo (in imitation of Luca Giordano); and, on the right-hand wall, *The Dream of St Joseph and the Conception,* by Rizi.

View of the Sacristy, the vault with frescoes by Luca Giordano.

There are also a number of other 16th- and 17th-century canvases of lesser importance.

The **Sacristy** was designed and built by Vergara the Younger around the end of the 16th century. On the vault, the Neapolitan Luca Giordano painted one of his grandiose frescoes in the closing years of the 17th century; this is *The Descent of the Virgin to Bestow the Chasuble on St Ildefons* and it includes the figures of *St Leocadia,* bishops, saints, virtues and angels. Giordano's speed as an artist earned him the nickname *fa presto* and he painted a large number of pictures in Spain. His self-por-

Don Duarte de Almeida, a Portuguese officer at the Battle of Toro.

A 17th-century door leads to the first square section of the chapel. In the west wall there are three niches with display cabinets and on the left three Neo-Classical Corinthian altarpieces of marble and bronze, designed by Ventura Rodríguez (1772) with paintings by Maella of *St James* in the centre and the *Adoration of the Magi* and the *Nativity* at the sides. Of the organs above, in the Plateresque gallery, one dates from 1654 and was made by Miguel Puche while the other dates from 1721. In the right-hand wall is a 17th-century *Immaculate Conception*. Opposite, a large pointed arch with Renaissance coffers and resting on pilasters decorated with grotesques leads to the main section of this chapel, which is enclosed by a fine screen by Céspedes.

The choir stalls, of walnut and dating from the 17th century, prove how important this chapel was with its twenty-six chaplains whose endowments, granted by John I in 1382, are perpetual, as are a further eight granted by Queen Catherine of Lancaster. In the two side walls, above the choir stalls, are the tombs of the Trastámara kings: on the right those of *Henry II* (d. 1379) and his wife *Doña Juana Manuel* (d. 1381), and on the left those of *Henry III the Sufferer* (d. 1407), and his wife *Catherine of Lancaster* (d. 1418), granddaughter of Peter I. All the effigies on these tombs are recumbent, date from the 14th century and came from the old chapel. They were carved by Luis González and Pedro Rodríguez. Also on the right-hand side is an orant of John II, by Juan de Borgoña; this is a commemorative statue as the king is actually buried in the Charterhouse of Miraflores in Burgos.

In the presbytery are the tombs with orants of *John I* (d. 1390) on the left, and his wife *Doña Leonor de Aragón* (d. 1382) on the right, carved in 1534 by Jorge Contreras, and situated here at Siloé's suggestion.

In contrast to the Plateresque style of the rest of the chapel, the rich marble and bronze altarpieces are Neo-Classical. The two at the sides, designed by Ventura Rodríguez (1777) with paintings by Maella are of *St Hermenegild* (left) and *St Ferdinand* (right). As the inscriptions state, the larger of the two was financed by Charles IV and designed by Mateo Medina in 1805. It displays angels, the royal coat of arms

Detail from the a fresco on the vault of the Sacristy, by Luca Giordano.

and figures of *SS. Peter and Paul* by Alfonso Bergaz; the painting of the *Descent* is by Maella. During the Neo-Classical reform Plateresque altarpieces by Berruguete, Comontes, Bernardino Bonifacio and Juan de Borgoña and the stained-glass windows by Juan de Ortega were lost.

Opposite the Chapel of Reyes Nuevos, on the pillar between the two side aisles, is a small altarpiece (between balustered columns) of the *Virgin and Child* dating from the first half of the 16th century.

23. The Chapel of Santa Leocadia. The 13th-century structure of this chapel is still intact. At the end of the 15th century it was enclosed with stonework of beautiful Flamboyant Gothic tracery imitating that made by Hanequín de Bruselas for the Chapel of Santiago but with Plateresque motifs, one being laurel leaves. The screen was made by a follower of Céspedes's in the 1540s, when alterations were made to the chapel by Bishop Ruiz de Ribera (d. 1539) for his own tomb and that of his uncle, Canon Juan Ruiz (d. 1535). The canvas of the Toledo martyr in a Vega landscape was painted by Ramón Seyro, a pupil of Maella's, and the frame is of various types of marble (1786).

24. The Chapel of El Cristo a La Columna, also known as the Chapel of *Los Estudiantes*, has retained its original architecture. The decoration is 15th-century Gothic, with a simple screen, stained-glass windows ascribed to Enrique Alemán and an altarpiece with wood-carvings of the *Christ on the Pillar*, *SS. Peter and John the Evangelist,* and, in the attic, a *La Verónica,* famous for a miracle which took place in 1469. On the right, another *Verónica* wood-carving with a painted *Holy Face* dates from the early-16th century.

On the pillar in front of the chapel is a small 16th-century altarpiece of the *Resurrection*.

25. The Entrance to the Sacristy was built in black marble by J. B. Monegro. Above the portal is the coat of arms of Cardinal Sandoval, who in 1612 renewed all the stones bearing a list of the prelates of the See since its foundation. These stones were arranged around the door, and until Mendoza bore the prelates' names only, with more than one name on each stone. Since Cisneros, each name appears individually and the information is more complete. The list continues until 1927.

trait is on one of the upper windows (the last on the left, apparently open). The late-Baroque version of the Gothic rail with figures leaning over it is also interesting.

Ignacio Haan's large marble and bronze *altarpiece* was commissioned by Cardinal Borbón in 1798. Carved by the sculptor Mariano Salvatierra and the marble-worker Aldobo, it was completed in 1803. Also interesting is *The Disrobing of Christ*, painted especially for this room by El Greco (1587). It depicts the moment before the crucifixion when the soldiers stripped Christ. Inspired by the Meditations of St Bonaventure, this masterpiece of the Cretan's is characteristic of the pious sensitivity of Mannerism, although its atypical composition gave rise to controversy among his contemporaries. Other paintings on the Sacristy walls by Theotocopoulus are: *Christ Blessing* and an *Apostolado* (one of his best); *St Peter in Tears; St Joseph* (the model taken from the painting in the Toledo chapel of the same name); *Christ on the Cross* (belonging to the Real Patronato del Colegio de Doncellas Nobles); and *St Francis at Prayer.*

Masterpieces in the Sacristy by other painters, starting with the wall on the right of the door, include: *Paul III*, a copy of Titian's work by Van Dyck; the *Entombment* by Giovanni Bellini; *St Agnes,* by Van Dyck; *The Appearance of St Leocadia to the King and St Ildefons* (1617), by Pedro Orrente; *St Sebastian*, by Luis Tristán; and *The Holy Family* (c. 1624) by Van Dyck. In the last niche on the right is *Christ on the Way to Calvary* by Francisco de Goya, and opposite this, in an identical marble frame, *Prayer in the Garden* by José Ramos (both commissioned in 1798). On either side of the altarpiece are *The Adoration of the Shepherds* and *The Adoration of the Magi,* both by Orrente. Furthermore, on the left side of the

The Disrobing of Christ, by Domenico Theotocopoulus — El Greco — in the Sacristy.

Sacristy, walking towards the entrance are: *The Flight into Egypt,* by Antiveduto Grammatica; *Christ on the Cross*, by Luis Tristán; *The Last Supper, St Ildefons and St Barbara,* by Juan de Borgoña; and *Christ and the Samaritan Woman*, by Giovanni Battista (il Cerano) Crespi. Of Roman alabaster, *the tomb of Cardinal Luis de Borbón* is a Neo-Classical work by Valeriano Salvatierra (1824), whose father Mariano carved

26. The Chapel and Antechapel of Nuestra Señora del Sagrario, patron saint of Toledo. The work on all this part of the Cathedral together with the Ochavo, the Sacristy and its adjacent rooms was begun in the time of Cardinal Quiroga and carried out mainly during the time of his successor Sandoval.

The whole project was designed in 1592 by Nicolás de Vergara the Younger. For its construction the Chapels of Santa Marina, San Agustín and San Andrés, and the adjacent Hospital del Rey were demolished. Work began in 1594 and the first stone was laid in 1595, shortly after Quiroga's death. Work was intensified in 1599 when Cardinal Sandoval became archbishop. When Vergara died in 1606 Monegro took over and by the time of his death in 1624 everything except the Ochavo — continued by Theotocopoulus and Juan Gómez de Mora — had been completed

Vergara's elegant classical architecture is splendid, being entirely faced with bronze (cast by Alejandro Bracci, Andrés Salinas and Francisco Sánchez) and marble from various points of origin — Genoa, Estremoz, Granada, San Pablo, Urda, Tortosa, Espejón, Carcabuey and Priego — which was brought in large blocks subsequently carved by Bartolomeo Aprille and Giambattista Semini. With frescoes by Eugenio Cajés and Vicente Carducho the room emulates the contemporary works of papal Rome.

In front of the entrance, the grave of Cardinal Portocarrero (d. 1709) is a Baroque contrast between the mundane greatness of the prelate — as seen in the sheer size of the copper plaque — and his disillusioned epitaph: "Here lies dust, ash and nothing [more]".

Of red and white marble, the **doorway** with its columns of the Composite order was made by Monegro (1610); an inscription states that it leads to the Reliquary and Treasury and to the burial chapel of Cardinal Sandoval y Rojas, whose coat of arms is displayed in the attic. Above this there are statues of the *Virgin, St Ildefons* and *St Bernard*. The screen was wrought by Bartolomé Rodríguez in 1616; the doors are of rare woods.

The Antechapel, also known as the Chapel of Santa Marina and the Chapel of Los Doctores (as it was stipulated that each of the seven chaplains endowed by Cardinal Sandoval must be a Doctor of one of the five principal universities in Spain or the University of Bologna), has a truncated dome with frescoes displaying grotesques

Christ on the Way to Calvary, by Francisco de Goya, on one of the side altars in the Sacristy.

by Carducho and Cajés. On the altar on the right is an *Ascension,* while on that on the left is *St Marina;* both are anonymous 17th-century Italian works. To the left of the latter, above the door leading to the sacristy, is a copy of Saraceni's *Descent* by Francisco Aguirre and painted in 1644. There is also a *St Lucy* by Agustín Navarro. The upper section of these two walls is also painted with frescoes by Carducho and Cajés: the *Adoration of the Magi* and the *Presentation* are in the centre, while at the sides are four sibyls. In this chapel's small sacristy, whose doorway is in the middle of the left-hand wall, is the epitaph of Pedro Pérez, one of the cathedral's first architects (d. 1291).

A large semi-circular arch with a screen by Francisco Sierra leads to the **Chapel of El Sagrario,** an area of grandiose elegance with a dome above. Formed by compound piers, the walls are faced with various types of marble, predominantly of dark and reddish tones in accordance with the funerary character of this chapel which was ceded by the Chapter to Archbishop Sandoval as a burial place for himself and members of his family; their coats of arms are displayed on the walls.

Between the two doors leading to the reliquary or ochavo is the **Altar of La Virgen del Sagrario**: the silver throne was designed by Sebastián de Herrera Barnuevo (1655) and made (1656-1674) by the Florentine goldsmith Virgilio Fanelli; its original wreathed columns were replaced by the fluted Composite ones when it was gilded in 1806. The image was originally situated above the altar, in the central area of the second section in a small niche of jasper and bronze with frescoes by Jiménez Donoso and Rizi and paintings on copper by F. del Po, all financed by Cardinal Pascual de Aragón. This Gothic image of Toledo's patron saint is of wood plated with silver.

The balcony opposite belongs to an oratory and chambers made by Cardinal Sandoval as a place of withdrawal for religious contemplation. These rooms lead to the Archbishop's Palace. The *St Fabian* and *St Sebastian* at the sides are by Carducho.

In the wall on the left-hand side is the tomb of Cardinal Sandoval y Rojas (d. 1618), while in that on the right are the tombs of his parents and three of his brothers. To the sides of these monuments are oratories, each with three paintings. On the left-hand side, the first displays *St Bernard, The Vision of St Bernard* and *The Virgin*

St Luke the Evangelist, by Domenico Theotocopoulus — El Greco — in the Sacristy.

St Peter in Tears, also by Domenico Theotocopoulus — El Greco — in the Sacristy.

most of the late 18th-century sculptures on both the interior and exterior of the Cathedral.

Other paintings are: *Cardinal Albergati,* ascribed to Carlo Coresa; the *Nativity, Adoration of the Magi,* and *Rest on the Flight into Egypt,* (1540-1545), all by Francisco Comontes; the *Presentation of the Child in the Temple,* by Luis de Velasco (1587); *David Playing the Harp,* Italian and painted in the 17th century after Domenichino's circle; the *Assumption,* by Carlo Maratta; and the *Adoration of the Magi,* by Francisco Rizi (1645).

The pictures in the upper section are by a number of painters (Antonio González Velázquez, José del Castillo, Andrés de la Calleja) who worked under Corrado Giaquinto. They were copied from originals by Luca Giordano for reproduction in tapestry form at the Real Fábrica in Madrid for the *Joseph, David and Solomon* series.

Of the sculptures, particularly important is Pedro de Mena's *St Francis* (1663). It is in a cabinet in one of the narrow spaces between columns (where goldwork items are also on display).

The cases next to the altar contain a number of interesting items: a 12th-century Romanesque casket of *St Eugenius;* a Byzantine soapstone dish, with reliefs depicting the *Twelve High Feast Days in the Liturgical Year* (10th century); the pillow, sword, crown and spurs of Sancho IV, dating from the 13th century and taken from his tomb in the Main Chapel (see p. 14); the slippers and spurs from the tomb of the Infante Don Pedro de Aguilar; two small Limoges enamelwork *reliquaries;* and a 14th-century *Reliquary of St Lucy* from Siena.

Adoring the Child, and the second the Martyrdom of St Eugenius, by Carlo Saraceni, the *Appearance of St Dionysius to Ercoldus* and the *Sermon of St Eugenius.* In the upper area of this wall are an *Assumption* and an *Annunciation.* Except for the painting by Saraceni, all are by Vicente Carducho and date from 1615.

On the right-hand side, the first oratory, which leads to the Sacristy, displays *St Leocadia in Prison* by Carlo Saraceni (c. 1613), the *Flagelation of St Leocadia* and *St Leocadia Before the Praetor* by Eugenio Cajés, and the second the *Descent,* by Carlo Saraceni, the *Miraculous Appearance of St Leocadia to St Ildefons and Recceswinth* and the *Sermon of St Ildefons,* by Eugenio Cajés. In the upper area are frescoes of the *Birth of the Virgin* and the *Immaculate Conception.* Except for the paintings by Saraceni, all the paintings on this side are by Eugenio Cajés and date from 1615.

In the third section, the windows are flanked by the *Eight Doctors of the Latin and Greek*

(Left) the Altar of Nuestra Señora del Sagrario, patron saint of Toledo, in her chapel. *

(Right) St Francis of Assisi, by Pedro de Mena, in the Sacristy.

Churches; the pendentives display prophets with archbishop-saints of Toledo — David and Eladio, Ezekiel and Julian, Solomon and Eulogio, Isaiah and Eugenius — all with verses alluding to the Virgin. On the dome are the *Four Evangelists.*

The great festivities celebrated on the solemn consecration of this chapel were attended by Philip III, the royal family and all the Court, who with the clergy formed an incredible procession through the city on 30th October 1616, the day when the image was placed in the new chapel.

The vestry

Adjacent to the Sacristy, this room was used as a changing area by the canons and prebendaries. It contains a number of very interesting pictures, including: the *Baptism of Christ,* in a curious imitation of Raphael's style by Luca Giordano; *Christ on the Cross,* by Titian; a copy of Diego Velázquez's *Cardinal Borja*; *Cardinal Borbón*, by Esteve; *The Mystical Betrothal of St Catherine,* a fine old copy of Rubens; *SS. Carlo Borromeo and Philip Neri,* by Guido Reni; the *Nativity,* by Jacopo Bassano; the *Presentation in the Temple*, by Francesco Bassano; *St Augustine* (1606), by Juan Pantoja de la Cruz; *St James of Alcalá*, by José de Ribera (1644); several vases of flowers by Mario dei Fiori and by Seghers. The paintings on the ceiling, by José Donoso and Claudio Coello, were commissioned by Cardinal Pascual de Aragón in 1671.

Cope of Archbishop Don Sancho de Aragón (13th century), in the Museum of Liturgical Vestments.

The museum of liturgical vestments

For reasons of space, it is not possible to discuss all the rich contents of this room here, but each item is clearly labelled. The first room, which housed the great processional monstrance, now contains: the cope of Archbishop Don Sancho de Aragón (13th century); Arab standards won by Alfonso XI at the Battle of Río Salado; processional cross covers, from the 16th to 18th centuries; a frontal and altar cloths embroidered with coral (17th-century Neapolitan).

The second room contains: chasubles, pluvial copes, dalmatics and choir capes, mainly from Toledo and dating from the 16th and 17th centuries. Here the visitor must try to imagine these inanimate objects, plus the fifteen capes worn by the Archbishop and Prebendaries, as vestments worn by members of the clergy moving to and fro between the Main Chapel and the choir during the services held in the Cathedral.

The imposing **Ochavo** is a major example of the most magnificent Spanish Baroque of the 17th century. Its walls were faced with different types of marble by Bartolomé Zumbigo according to plans by Pedro de la Torre. They are divided up into niches for the sumptuous **reliquaries:** from its function as the treasury (*sacrum aerarium*) which occupied this area of the Cathedral in the Middle Ages comes the Spanish name *Sagrario*. The name, however, gives no more than a suggestion of the incredible collection of gold items it contains, particularly important being the arks of St Eugenius and St Leocadia and the Maundy Thursday monument. The original frescoes on the dome by Carreño and Rizi were replaced in 1778 by others painted by Maella. Opposite the Chapel of El Sagrario are the small altarpieces of *St Francis* and *St Dominic*.

(Right) set of three copes commissioned by Cardinals Mendoza and Cisneros, in the Museum of Liturgical Vestments.

(Below) the 18th-century mechanism of the clock above the north transept doorway.

27. The Puerta del Reloj takes its name ("Door of the Clock") from its clock, which regulated the various Cathedral activities connected with worship. The current mechanism dates from the 18th century but the clock has existed at least since the 16th century, when Diego de Velasco and Juan de Tovar made its Plateresque adornment (1536-45), painted by Francisco Comontes. The bells were beaten by two mace-bearers carved by Diego Copín. From the same period are the *Annunciation,* by Nicolás de Vergara the Elder and J. B. Vázquez, and the circular relief of the *Appearance of St Leocadia*, by Gregorio Bigarny (1542). On two smaller medallions, which are also circular, J. B. Vázquez depicted the prophets Samuel and Zechariah.

The great **rose window** with a crucifix in the centre surrounded by prophets and saints contains the Cathedral's oldest stained-glass, dating from the late-13th and early-14th centuries; the glass at the sides dates from the 15th century.

The treasury

The Cathedral's goldwork was always kept in the Sacrarium and, from the 17th century, in the *Ochavo,* where most of it is still to be found. However, as access to this area was difficult for liturgical reasons and also for security, the Chapel of La Torre (see p. 10) was adapted in 1900 to house a selection of the most important items for exhibition.

Particularly interesting in this respect is another of Cardinal Cisneros's great achievements — the grandiose *processional Monstrance.* The ostensory or small monstrance in the centre dates from the late-

The Corpus Christi processional monstrance, made by Enrique de Arfe (1515-1524), in the Treasury.

The crown of the Virgen del Sagrario, patron saint of Toledo, in the Treasury.

Flanking the door are pictures of the *Stories of Solomon, David and Joseph*, by Luca Giordano; copies under the direction of Corrado Giaquinto were made of them for the tapestry room in the *Real Palacio* in Madrid. The canvases of *St Thomas Aquinas* and *St Gertrude* date from the 17th century.

The wood-carving on the doors imitating the Plateresque style of the Puerta de los Leones (see p. 22) was executed by Raimundo Capuz around 1712.

On its east front, the **transept** has galleries and Gothic triforia in which during the week following the anniversary of a victory, the standards taken from the enemy in battles, e.g. Las Navas de Tolosa, the Salado, Toro, Lepanto, Nordlingen, Almansa, etc, and donated to the cathedral by the victorious monarch, were hung.

On the pillar between the transept and the Chapel of El Sagrario is a small altarpiece with a picture of *St Peter of Alcántara* painted in 1789 by Maella. Opposite it, the altarpiece of the *Virgin with Saints and Donor* dates from the first half of the 16th century.

The first pillar where the end of the two side-aisles meets the north transept (looking towards the west end of the Cathedral) is known as the Pillar of *La Lavandera*. This was once the site for a chest (on a marble pedestal) in which foundlings were left and also for the collecting box for alms given to the Hospital de Santa Cruz, where such children were brought up. There are two small Plateresque altarpieces on this pillar, one dedicated to a Dominican Saint and the other to St Bernard.

The gallery above the inner side aisle and opposite the Neo-Classical organ overlooks the high altar and choir; it was built so that the kings could follow the services when they came to the Cathedral and was later used by the Archbishop and his retinue for the same purpose.

28. The Chapel of San Pedro was built in 1415 by Alvar Martínez to serve as a parish church for the Cathedral neighbourhood and also as a funeral chapel for Archbishop Sancho de Rojas (1422), who financed it: the Archbishop's epitaph is written in cartouches among the thistle leaf ornamentation on the jambs of the Gothic front. Above the uppermost archivolt are busts of Archbishop Rojas and the fourteen *dignidades* of the Toledo choir, each identified by his post.

15th century; apparently Isabella the Catholic ordered it to be made with the first gold to reach Spain from the Americas. A work of incredible sensitivity, it is ascribed to Pedro Vigil or Friar Juan de Segovia. Cisneros purchased it on the death of the queen and in 1515 commissioned Enrique de Arfe with a small Gothic temple (1517-1524) — designed like a cathedral spire two and a half metres tall — for the ostensory to be kept in. Although it is known that Copín and Juan de Borgoña made maquettes and drawings for the temple, it is not known if these influenced Arfe's final work. In 1594, when Francisco Merino was commissioned by Archbishop Quiroga to gild it, it was found to consist of 5,600 pieces held together by 12,500 screws. At this time the coats of arms of Cisneros, Fonseca, Quiroga and those of the works canons were included with explanatory cartouches on the twelve sides of the base. It displays 250 small figures, among these an enamelled

The monstrance pedestal, designed by Narciso Tomé and carved by the silversmith M. Vargas Machuca.

Christ Risen in the centre of the second section, and a *Christ Child* in the third, while angels and small bells are suspended from the arches. It is surmounted with a cross of diamonds added in 1600. Except for the pedestal — which dates from the time of the Infante Cardinal Don Luis Antonio de Borbón (mid-18th century), and was designed by Narciso Tomé and made by Manuel Vargas Machura — this extremely impressive piece is paraded through the streets on the solemn feast of Corpus Christi.

The Bible presented to Alfonso X in 1258 — the *Biblia de San Luis* — is a major work from the French royal miniatures workshop. The customs and dress of the 13th century are depicted in its five thousand scenes (almost all of which are on gold backgrounds) and seven hundred and fifty miniatures. Made up of three volumes, it is one of the "moralist bibles", so-called as it relates the passages from the New Testament to those from the Old.

Particularly interesting among the remaining items (made of silver unless otherwise indicated) are the following: three *trays with scenes from the life of Alexander the Great* (18th century, a gift from Cardinal Lorenzana); a 15th-century Gothic *reliquary of St Leocadia* in the form of a ship, ascribed to Juan González de Madrid; a *tray depicting the*

Above these are *St Peter Enthroned.* All of these sculptures date from the 15th century. The *Choice of St Peter* and *The Freeing of St Peter* are frescoes ascribed to Pedro Berruguete and dating from the end of the 15th century. Other frescoes painted by Berruguete and Comontes inside this chapel and in the cloisters are now lost due to damp. In the interior of the chapel, the large windows of the apse with trefoil tracery date from the beginning of the 15th century, while those in the nave were remade with Flamboyant tracery by Hanequín de Bruselas in the middle of the same century. The window on the left was walled in when Cisneros erected the upper cloisters.

The five Neo-Classical marble altarpieces date from the time of Lorenzana: the largest displays a canvas by Francisco Bayeu depicting *St Peter Healing the Cripple*, the two closest to the pres-

The doorway to the Chapel of San Pedro, by Alvar Martínez (1415). *

bytery are of *St Peter of Osma* and *St Julian of Cuenca,* also by Bayeu, while the smallest two are of *St Ignatius Loyola* and *St Francis Xavier* and were painted by Agustín Esteve. These last four paintings were commissioned by Archdeacon Matías de Robles in 1788. The stalls were made by Germán López around 1770. Above these, on the left, is the tomb of the chapel's founder, Archbishop Sancho de Rojas. Canon Juan de Vergara, the Toledo historian whose pseudonym was Pedro de Alcocer, also lies here. Above the entrance is the choir, with a stone parapet of Gothic tracery and an organ whose wooden case imitating marble and wood-carving dates from the 18th century. Above this is the Archbishop's gallery, which leads directly to his Palace.

29. The Puerta de Santa Catalina was built in the 14th century when Tenorio was archbishop and at the same time as the Cloisters. Until the 16th century, when the Puerta de la Presentación was built (see p. 56), it was the only door from the Cloisters to the Cathedral. Hanequín de Bruselas made alterations to it in the mid-15th century, including lobulated and depressed ogee arches, complex tracery, canopies and vegetal decoration typical of the Flamboyant Gothic style. It seems that the *Coronation* group of figures dates from the 15th century and came originally from the Puerta de los Leones. The statues behind are remains of the 14th-century ornamentation.

30. The Chapel of La Piedad was founded by Canon Alfonso Martínez in the 15th century. Alterations were made to the façade in 1716. The altarpiece of *St Teresa*, which dates from the mid-17th century and gives this chapel its present name, came originally from the Chapel of San Ildefonso and was placed here at the beginning of this century. The chapel is therefore Baroque, although it contains a fragment of stone with rich Gothic decoration and a 13th-century tomb, as well as a wood-carving of the Virgin to whom it was formerly dedicated — the *Virgen de la Piedad;* this statue, on a 17th-century console in the right-hand corner, dates from the 15th century.

At the sides are the small altarpieces of the *Ecce Homo* and *St Judas Thaddaeus*, both dating from the 18th century.

Rape of the Sabine Women, by Matías Melinc (16th century); a *Cross of rock crystal,* dating from the second half of the 16th century; the *Cross of Cardinal Tavera;* a 15th-century Gothic *ship* of silver and rock crystal; a *Cross* of rock crystal and silver, by Tavera; a *Crown of the Virgin of the Sacrarium* (1641), by Francisco Salinas and Andrés Bejerano; the *boat* of St Blas, dating from the 14th century and donated by Tenorio (the upper section was made in the 16th century).

(Left) view of the cloisters and the Torre de las Campanas.

(Below) the Capilla Bautismal with its screen by Domingo de Céspedes.*

31. The Capilla Bautismal. Archbishop Cerezuela commissioned Hanequín (who had built his family chapel, see p.p. 34, 36) to make the elaborate Flamboyant Gothic **faces** of this chapel (c. 1450). With certain variations the entrance to the Cloisters repeated the same plan as that of the nave, where there are sculptures of the Evangelists under canopies rising to the high pinnacles. The very pointed ogee arch displays symbols of the Passion and, above, angels. The magnificent screen is the only one made by Domingo de Céspedes with figures — some decorative, others forming the scene of the Baptism — and also bears the coats of arms of Fonseca and the Churchwarden López de Ayala (1524). Of a style between Gothic and Renaissance, the **font** and its cover in the shape of an ovolo, is profusely decorated with volutes, leaves, fruit and figures of children, all in bronze. It dates from the late-15th or early-16th century. Beneath a Flamboyant gable in a large niche in the right-hand wall is the altarpiece with the

THE CLOISTERS

The cloisters were built by Alvar González during Archbishop Pedro Tenorio's pontificate. In the process, it was necessary to relocate a market and a Jewish neighbourhood. As a burial place for himself, Tenorio also erected the *Chapel of San Blas*, having it painted with fine trecentist frescoes; the altarpieces were painted in 1592 by Luis de Velasco. For some years the chapel has been closed to the public.

As Cervantes recalls in *Don Quixote*, the cloisters were often used by members of the upper classes for strolling through. In the 15th century this area was decorated with mural paintings by Pedro Berruguete and other artists. As these had fallen into a sad state of repair by the end of the 18th century, Cardinal Lorenzana and the Chapter commissioned Francisco Bayeu and Mariano Salvador Maella to paint a new series (1776-1787), some of which have been lost and others very seriously damaged due to damp. They were dedicated to the saints of Toledo — Leocadia, Eugenius, Casilda, Eladio, Eulogio, Julian, Ildefons and the Child of La Guardia. The sketches for them (in the Cathedral Museum), allow us to see how those paintings which are now lost once looked; they also

The upper gallery in the cloisters, at the "Las Claverías" level.

Calvary; the Christ dates from the beginning of the 15th century and the Virgin and St John were carved by Francisco de Amberes in 1507. The panels with scenes from the Gospel at the bottom of the altarpiece were painted in the late-14th or early-15th century by an Italian or an italianized Spaniard who was working on the pictures then being painted in the Chapel of San Blas. On the left-hand wall are three painted wood-carvings: the *Virgin and Child* is Gothic and dates from the first half of the 14th century, while the *Angels* on either side were carved by Francisco de Amberes in 1507.

32. The Chapel of La Virgen de La Antigua. Abutting the pillar this chapel is a beautiful example of Flamboyant architecture in gilded and painted stone; it dates from the end of the 15th century and is very similar to the work of Diego Copín. It has elegant arches with pinnacles. The image from which it takes its name dates from the beginning of the 15th century.

Its founders were the first Duke and Duchess of Maqueda, Gutierre de Cárdenas, an important counsellor to the Catholic Kings, and his wife Teresa Enríquez, whose piety won her the nickname of "the Madwoman of the Sacrament"; she is buried in one of the chapels she founded in Torrijos (province of Toledo). The statues of the couple are in a kneeling position. They were painted in Toledo at the beginning of the 16th century and the panels of the *Birth of the Virgin* (by Juan de Borgoña), the *Mass of St Gregory* and the *Descent* were placed below them. The screen was made by Alonso de Zamora in 1634.

33. The Chapel of Doña Teresa de Haro is named after its founder, the wife of the Marshall of Castile, Diego López de Padilla, whose son was the Toledo *comunero* Padilla. Their arms — with three frying-pans — gave rise to the name "Christ of the Ladles" by which the chapel was also known. The crucifix was made by Ignacio Alonso (1706) and presides over an 18th-century Baroque altarpiece, above which the tracery of the large window overlooking the cloisters is visible. In the side walls are beautiful Gothic niches, and the right-hand wall displays a *Seizure of Christ*, painted in Toledo in the 17th century. The Gothic front with its triple basket-handle arch highly decorated with thistles and openwork crenellation, dates from the late-15th century. The screen was made by Master Pablo around 1480.

confirm that plans were made to replace the Gothic portals leading to the old summer Chapter House and certain other rooms with new Neo-Classical ones but that this was fortunately not done.

It was Cisneros who erected the upper cloisters and the staircase known as El Tenorio, the former being a simple, flat, functional structure intended to force the canons to live together as a community under the same roof. This proved, however, to be one of the few schemes of Cisneros's to fail, for the area was converted into dwellings for the lay staff and also into storerooms known as the Claverías and Sala de los Gigantones — names which conjure up the day-to-day life of the Cathedral as described by Galdós (*Angel Guerra)* and Blasco Ibáñez (*La Catedral*). There have been countless references to the Cathedral by travellers and writers, but it is worth remembering that it is here where the narrator of *Don Quixote* obtained the manuscripts on which he based his story.

THE EXTERIOR OF THE CATHEDRAL

The door known as the *Puerta del Mollete* was built at the beginning of the 15th century, its name coming from a type of bread roll given by the Chapter as alms. It leads out into the square containing the *Archbishop's Palace* and the *Ayuntamiento* or City Council building. Begun around 1418 under the supervision of Alvar Gómez, the **Cathedral's main façade** stands opposite these buildings. The upper section in front of the rose window was built during the alterations made to the

Cathedral in the 17th century, although the entire façade was subsequently restored (1787) by Eugenio Durango. The main façade is flanked by the tower known as the **Torre de las Campanas** on the left (begun by Alvar Gómez and completed by Hanequín), and the chapel known as the Capilla Mozárabe on the right.

In the centre, the **Portada del Perdón** entrance displays sculptures of the *Twelve Apostles* on the jambs, the *Saviour* on the central pillar and the *Descent* on the tympanum. Above is a *Last Supper* by Mariano Salvatierra. The *door panels* themselves date from 1337 and are completely covered with sheets of bronze displaying reliefs of castles, lions and geometric and vegetal decoration all surrounded by inscriptions invoking the Virgin. Above the central pillar in front of the rose window is an allegory on *Religion*. On both sides of the door are large pillars with sculptures of saints, patriarchs, prophets, kings and archbishops. The two **side doorways** do not have sculptures on their jambs, although their archivolts display heads of saints and angels. The

(Left) the Torre de las Campanas, by Alvar Gómez and Hanequín (15th century).

(Right) the Puerta del Reloj, otherwise known as the Puerta de la Chapinería and the Puerta de la Feria at the end of the north transept.

34. The Puerta del Arzobispo is used by the Archbishop and his retinue as they go down to the choir through an arch connecting the Palace with the Cathedral. The passageway, the staircase and the doors were all begun by Vergara the Younger and completed by Monegro (1601-10), in the time of Sandoval. The three anonymous 17th-century canvases with dark marble frames depict *St Carlo Borromeo, St Vincent*

Apostles on the jambs of the Puerta del Perdón, in the middle of the main façade.

Ferrer and the *Appearance of the Child Jesus to St Antony.*

35. The Puerta de La Presentación. This door leads from the Cloisters to the first section of the side aisles. Made by Alonso de Covarrubias in 1565, its Plateresque outer façade harmonises with both the style of the cloisters — which is Gothic — and that of the interior, which is closer to Classicism. Two fluted Corinthian columns, whose lower third sections (like the pedestals and jambs) are adorned with grotesques, flank a semi-circular arch with a keystone displaying a small relief of the *Descent;* above, and within the curved tympanum, is the *Eternal Father,* by Martínez Castañeda. The door panels were made by Monegro in 1601.

This door cannot have been made before this doorway on the right is known both as the *Portada del Juicio* and the *Portada de los Escribanos,* while that on the left has three different names — *Portada del Infierno*, *Portada de las Palmas,* and *Portada de la Torre*. Over each side doorway are five niches containing statues of saints (18th century) and, above them, a number of galleries with semi-circular arches between Ionic demi-columns.

At each end of the Lonja forecourt, which is enclosed by iron railings and hewn stone pillars, are sculptures by Domingo Díaz and Cristóbal de Herencia, one being of *St Eugenius* and the other of *St Ildefons.* On more than one occasion during the 16th and 17th centuries, the whole of this façade was refaced with sumptuous though short-lived ornamentation, one example being that designed by Diego de Alcántara to receive the relics of St Leocadia in 1587.

Circling the beautiful Gothic dome of the Chapel known as the *Capilla Mozárabe* (designed by Antón Egas in 1509 and surmounted with a lantern by Jorge Manuel Theotocopoulus), we come to the door known as the *Puerta Llana,* a beautiful Neo-Classical Ionic propylaeum by Ignacio Haan (1800). The next door, at the end of the south transept, is known as the **Puerta de los Leones** (also called *Puerta Nueva*

(Left) the Puerta de los Leones or Puerta de la Alegría, at the end of the south transept.

(Right) the dome of the Capilla Mozárabe, by Enrique Egas and Jorge Manuel Theotocopoulus.

and Puerta de la Alegría). It was carved between 1460 and 1466, when Carrillo was archbishop, by a team of architects and sculptors from Flanders who included Egas Cueman, Juan Guas and Juan Alemán. It contains the *Apostles* and the *Virgin* on the central pillar However, the *Assumption of the Virgin*, other sculptures above these and the eleven medallions with prophets above the arch were carved by Salvatierra during the general restoration of the entrances made by the architect Eugenio Durango around 1780. The bronze-plated doors with their

late date as until 1534 the first two sections of the side aisle next to the cloisters were occupied by the original Chapel of Reyes Nuevos (see p. 38), which Cardinal Tavera had removed.

36. The Portal of the Chapel of La Torre was also built as a result of the removal of the Chapel of Reyes Nuevos, since its sacristy occupied the tower's ground floor, where Tavera created a new chapel dedicated to St John the Baptist. This magnificent doorway (1536), carved by a number of masons under Alonso de Covarrubias, including Gregorio Bigarny and Jamete, combined features from different styles: Gothic in the section immediately below the semi-circular arch with the statues of *SS. Paul, Ildefons, John* (left), *James, Eugenius, Peter* (right); Plateresque on the front — a medallion on the tympanum with a bust of *St John* by Gregorio Pardo (1537); and, in the ornamentation above and around the group, a *Quo Vadis* in painted baked clay by

Details from the upper section of the Torre de las Campanas, by Hanequín de Bruselas.

Cristóbal de Olarte (1523), plus the Emperor's coat of arms (above) with those of Cardinal Tavera and the Churchwarden, López de Ayala, at the sides. Since the beginning of this century the chapel has housed the cabinets containing the Cathedral's treasures (see p. 48). Particularly interesting also is the ceiling with prism ornamentation, transferred from the old Chapel of Reyes Nuevos by Juan de Orozco in 1540. The chapel was completed and the altarpieces carved during the time of Carranza, Tavera's successor.

On this tour, each and every work of art reminds us of the power of the institutions, clergy and nobles who commissioned it. Every altar brings to mind all the services and ceremonies and the *thirty-six thousand masses* celebrated here each year by the countless members of the clergy who lived from the Cathedral's revenues. But of the staff whose livelihood was the Cathedral and who brought the building to life — the vergers, bell-ringers, etc. — testimony also remains. For example, in four different places there are ancient chairs of walnut — at the entrance to the Sacristy, next to

superb knockers are masterpieces by Francisco de Villalpando, who was commissioned to make them in 1551; as he died before completing them, they were finished by his brother, Rui Díaz del Corral, some time before 1564. The iron grille was made by Juan Alvarez in 1646.

A walk around the Cathedral's tortuous east end is well worth the trouble for, having circled the *Chapter House* and its adjacent rooms, we come to the exterior of the castle-like Chapels of *San Ildefonso* and *Santiago* and the picturesque top of the *Transparente* window. Skirting the sober architecture (reminiscent of El Escorial) of the Casa del Tesorero, the Sacristy, the Ochavo and the Sacrarium, we come to the door known as the **Puerta del Reloj** at the end of the north transept. As this door dates from the beginning of the 14th century, it is the Cathedral's oldest. It was also known by two other names — Puerta de la Chapinería and Puerta de la Feria, as the street leading to it was once the place where Toledo's women's footwear *(chapines)* manufacturers worked and it was also used as a market or fair *(feria)* held after the Assumption in the middle of August. It was also known as *Puerta de los Reyes* ("Door of the Magi") and *Puerta del Niño Perdido* ("Door of the Lost Child") as these two themes are among the Gospel scenes from the Life of Christ and the Mother of God which adorn the tympanum in various sections — the childhood of Jesus at the bottom, his life as a public figure in the two sections in the middle, and the Death of the Virgin at the top. Such an extraordinary profusion of iconography is closely connected with the Mozarabic liturgy and the mystery plays. Prominent in one such relief, depicting the Marriage in Cana, are the large containers from which another name for this door — *Puerta de las Ollas* or "Door of the Pots" — was taken. The jambs

(Left) the main façade with the Perdón, Juicio and Infierno doorways.

(Right) the buttresses of the domes over the nave.

the Chapel of La Torre door, between the chapels of San Eugenio and San Martín, and between those of Reyes Viejos and Santa Ana. It was from these that the "presbyter guards" known as the "Silver Rods" due to the metal of the staffs they carried, watched over the Cathedral, while the "secular guards", for a similar reason known as the "Wooden Rods", had chairs next to the Puerta de los Leones and at the side of the *Capilla Bautismal*.

display eight sculptures of saints by Juan Alemán which date from the middle of the 15th century. The bronze doors were made in 1713 by Antonio Zurreño and J. A. Domínguez in imitation of Villalpando's Puerta de los Leones. The upper section of this façade was restored by Durango; on the left once stood the 15th-century clock tower — condemned and demolished in 1889. Originally made by Master Pablo (1482) for the Chapel of San Pedro, the *grille* over the atrium was transferred here in the 18th century.

BIBLIOGRAPHY

AMADOR DE LOS RIOS, R: *Monumentos arquitectónicos de España.* Toledo. Madrid 1905.

ARCO, Ricardo del: *Sepulcros de la Casa Real de Castilla*, Madrid 1954.

ARELLANO GARCIA, M: *La Capilla mozárabe o del Corpus Christi*, Toledo 1980.

ARRIBAS, F.: "Noticias sobre las capillas antigua y nueva de Reyes Nuevos en la Catedral de Toledo", *B.S.E.A.A.V.*, XI (1944-1945), p.p. 205-207.

AYALA MALLORY, Nina: "El Transparente de la Catedral de Toledo (1721-1732)", *Archivo Español de Arte,* no 167 (1969), p. 255 ff.

AZCARATE RISTORI, José María de: *La arquitectura gótica toledana del siglo XV,* Madrid 1958.

AZCARATE RISTORI, José María de: *Arte gótico en España,* Madrid 1990. Contains all Azcarate Ristori's most relevant previous bibliography on Hanequín, Egas and Guas.

BONILLA MORENO, G.: *Los órganos de la catedral de Toledo*, Toledo 1955, p. 119.

CABRERA DELGADO SILVEIRA, Antonio, and VELASCO, Pedro: *La catedral de Toledo* (guía del visitante), Cuenca 1983.

CASAS GOMEZ, Ignacio de las: *El conocimiento de la Arquitectura en la Catedral de Toledo*, tesis doctoral inédita dirigida por D. Julio Vidaurre, E.T.S.A.M., Madrid 1992.

CASTAÑEDA, Francisco Javier de: *Relación de los solemnes aparatos... con que... se celebró la colocación de Christo Sacramentado... a el Nuevo Magnífico Transparente.* Toledo, 1732.

CHECA CREMADES, Fernando: *Pintura y escultura del Renacimiento en España.* Cátedra, Madrid 1950.

CHUECA GOITIA, Fernando: *Arquitectura del siglo XVI,* "Ars Hispaniae", XI Madrid 1953.

CHUECA GOITIA, Fernando: *La catedral de Toledo,* León 1978.

CONRAD, Guido: "El ábside de la Catedral de Toledo", *Archivo Español de Arte,* no 190-191 (1975), p. 218.
CONRAD, Guido: "La Catedral de Toledo y la concepción del volumen en la estructura gótica", *Estudios e investigaciones,* Madrid, yearl, no 4, Oct. 1976.

DIEZ DEL CORRAL, Rosario: "La Catedral de Toledo como panteón: la capilla de San Eugenio", *Goya,* no 197, 1987, p.p. 274-277.

DIEZ DEL CORRAL, Rosario: *Arquitectura y mecenazgo. La imagen de Toledo en el Renacimiento.* Alianza Editorial, Madrid 1988.

DOMINGUEZ RODRIGUEZ, Ana: "El testamento de Alfonso X y la Catedral de Toledo", *Reales Sitios,* no 82 (1984).

DURAN SEMPERE, Agustín and AINAUD DE LASARTE: *Escultura gótica*, "Ars Hispaniae", tome VIII, Madrid 1956.

FRANCO MATA, Angela: "El génesis y el éxodo en la cerca exterior del coro de la catedral de Toledo", *Toletum,* Toledo, LXX, no 21, (1987), p.p. 53-160.

FRANCO MATA, Angela: "El periodo gótico"

GOMEZ MORENO, Manuel: *Las águilas del Renacimiento español.* Madrid, 1941.

HERRERA, Pedro de: *Descripción de la Capilla de Nuestra Señora del Sagrario*, Madrid 1617.

KUBLER, George: *Arquitectura de los siglos XVII y XVIII,* "Ars Hispaniae", XIV Madrid 1957.

LAMBERT, Elie: *El arte gótico en España*, Madrid 1931.

MARIAS, Fernando: *La arquitectura del Renacimiento en Toledo* (1541-1631), Madrid 1986.

MATEO GOMEZ, Isabel: Temas profanos en la escultura gótica española. Las sillerías de coro, Madrid 1979.

MATEO GOMEZ, Isabel: *La sillería baja de la catedral de Toledo,* Toledo 1982.

MINGARRO, Francisco, LOPEZ AZCONA, Concepción, et al.: "Estudios realizados en la Catedral de Toledo con vistas a su restauración y a la consolidación de sus materiales pétreos", *Congreso internacional de rehabilitación del Patrimonio Arquitectónico y edificación,* Canary Islands 1992. Other studies by the same team on the state of the Cathedral's stonework in Revista de la Sociedad Geológica de España, 6 (1993), p.p. 7-17.

NICOLAU CASTRO, Juan: "Las esculturas italianas del Transparente de la Catedral de Toledo", *Archivo Español de Arte*, no 273 (1996), p.p. 98-106.

NIETO ALCAIDE, Víctor: "El maestro Enrique Alemán, vidriero de las catedrales de Sevilla y Toledo", *Archivo Español de Arte*, XL 1967, p.p. 72-81.

NIETO ALCAIDE, Víctor: *La vidriera del Renacimiento en España,* Madrid 1970.

NIETO ALCAIDE, Víctor: *La luz, símbolo y sistema visual. El espacio y la luz en el arte gótico y del Renacimiento.* Madrid, 1978.

OLAGUER-FELIU, Fernando: *Las rejas de la Catedral de Toledo*, Toledo 1980.

PARRO, Sixto Ramón: *Toledo en la mano.* Tome I. Toledo, 1857. Ed. facs., Toledo 1978. Based on Pérez Sedano's work, although no acknowledgment is made; still an essential work.

PEREZ HIGUERA, Mª Teresa: *La puerta del reloj en la Catedral de Toledo,* Toledo 1987.

PEREZ SEDANO, Francisco: *Datos documentales inéditos para la Historia del Arte Español,* I: Notas del Archivo de la Catedral de Toledo redactadas en el siglo XVIII por el canónigo... Ed. de Elías Tormo, Madrid 1914. The essential printed source.

PIQUERO LOPEZ, Blanca: *La pintura gótica toledana anterior a 1450.* Toledo 1982.

PONZ, Antonio: *Viaje de España,* tome I, 3rd ed., Madrid 1787.

PRADOS, José María: "Las trazas del Transparente y otros dibujos de Narciso Tomé para la Catedral de Toledo", *Archivo Español de Arte*, no 196 (1976), p. 387 ff.

REVUELTA TUBINO, Matilde (coord.): *Inventario artístico de Toledo.* Tomeo II: la Catedral Primada. II vols, Ministerio de Cultura, Madrid 1983. With a complete bibliography.

RIVERA RECIO, J.F.: *Los arzobispos de Toledo en la Baja Edad Media (siglos XII-XV)*, Toledo 1969.

Various authors : *El Toledo de El Greco,* Exhibition catalogue, Ministerio de Cultura, Toledo 1982.

Various authors: *Rutas de Toledo*. Electa, Madrid 1993, p.p. 119-157.

Various authors : (PERIS SANCHEZ, Diego, coord.): *Arquitecturas de Toledo.* Junta de comunidades de Castilla-La Mancha, Toledo 1992, p.p. 409-479. The situation today, with a competent bibliography.

This book, published by Aldeasa, was printed in Madrid
on 27th November 1997, feast of St. Facundo,
at Estudios Gráficas Europeos

Lower choir stalls: The Conquest of Granada

Stall	**Archbishop's Choir** Carved by *Rodrigo Alemán*	**Dean's Choir** Carved by *Rodrigo Alemán*
1	Believed to be Granada	Believed to be Malaga
2		Nixar
3		
4	Altora	
5	Melis	
6	Xornas	Padux
7	Erejan	
8	Alminia	
9	Baza	Vera
10	Málaga	Huéscar
11	Málaga	Guadix
12	Salobreña	Purchena
13	Almuñécar	Almería
14	Comares	Rión
15	Vélez	Castilferro
16	Montefrío	Cambril
17	Moclín	Zaganí
18	Illora	Castul
19	Loja	Gor
20	Cazarabonela	Camoría
21	Coín	Moxácar
22	Cartama	Vélez el Blanco
23	Marbella	Gurarca
24	Ronda	Vélez el Rubio
25	Setenil	Soreo
26	Alora	Cabrera
27	Alhama	Almeria

Here sat the canons known as the *extravagantes*, the choir and Haro chaplains, and the salaried singers, the latter in front of lecterns.

The carvings, by *Rodrigo Alemán* (1495), depict the capture of various Andalusian cities during the conquest of the Muslim Kingdom of Granada by the Catholic Kings (1482-1492). The earliest battles are listed on the archbishop's side and closest to the screen. The names of the battles indicated in the carvings are transcribed here with their original spelling. A few stalls do not display names and these have been left blank.